The
Hidden
Miracle

Catherine Smith
&
Anna Kranz

Trust in the LORD!
Blessings,

Catherine

Scripture quotations are from The Holy Bible, English Standard Version®
(ESV®), copyright © 2001 by Crossway, a publishing ministry of Good
News Publishers. Used by permission. All rights reserved.

Permission for using the lyrics for "The Steadfast Love of
the Lord" was obtained by Celebration Copyright

ISBN: 978-1-4834-1703-5 (sc)
ISBN: 978-1-4834-1702-8 (e)

Library of Congress Control Number: 2014914934

Lulu Publishing Services rev. date: 10/31/2014

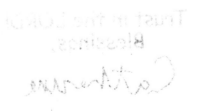

To Jesus Christ,
the Giver and Preserver of my life,
and the One who put the desire in my heart to share my story.

To Betsy,
my teacher-friend,
who shared many special times with me!
You knew, that tragic morning, that something
was wrong and came to find me.

To Terry,
my brother,
who helped Betsy find me and who got the emergency help I needed.

To Roberta, my mother,
To Cindy, my sister,
who both sensed in their hearts early in the morning of April 2, 1999,
that I was not well, and were praying for me even
before they knew what had happened.

To Gerald and Roberta, my parents,
To R.J., Cindy, and Terry, my siblings,
for loving me and for sharing the gift of life together.

To Anna,
my niece,
who made the sharing of this story possible. Without you I could
never have written this book. You understood my limited thoughts
and sentences, put them into written words, and made the story flow
and come alive! It's been a special journey of writing together.

I waited patiently for the Lord; he inclined to me and heard my cry.
He drew me up from the pit of destruction, out of the miry bog, and
set my feet upon a rock, making my steps secure. He put a new song
in my mouth, a song of praise to our God. Many will see and fear,
and put their trust in the Lord. Blessed is the man who makes the
Lord his trust, who does not turn to the proud, to those who go astray
after a lie! You have multiplied, O Lord my God, your wondrous
deeds and your thoughts toward us; none can compare with you! I
will proclaim and tell of them, yet they are more than can be told.
—Psalm 40:1–5

Catherine M. Smith

To my Lord and Savior, Jesus Christ,
The Author of my life story.
I praise You, Lord, for creating me with
a special passion for writing
and for giving me this opportunity to be a coauthor with my aunt.
May You receive the glory!

To my parents and siblings,
Tom and Cindy, Christina, Jonathan, Teresa, Caleb, Matthias,
Timothy, and Andrew,
and my many other dear friends and relatives
who prayed for this endeavor and took interest in it.

To all those who read this book
who are walking through life's joys and sorrows.
My prayer for you is that you, too, may find the
hidden miracles along the journey.
May you see that it is the gracious, loving
hand of the Lord writing your story
for the purpose of drawing you to Himself—to know Him!

Anna E. Kranz

Foreword

I like stories. I like books. And I love a book that leaves me better for having read it. This book fits that category. It is nonfiction that takes our emotions for a ride and takes our faith on a precious journey.

Catherine Smith, the central figure in the story, shares her unfolding drama, enriched by the responses and reactions of faithful family and friends. She lives her life not withdrawing from relationships because of her loss and limitations, but in community. She shares the lessons learned, the wisdom gained, and the faith strengthened by God in the midst of trials. The fellowship surrounding her is one of strong prayer commitment, love that holds on, and faith in the God they know well.

The coauthor of the book is Anna Kranz, who has been her aunt Catherine's assistant in presenting this testimony, first in spoken words and now in written form. She has skillfully interweaved the memories of family and friends, beginning with a traumatic event in 1999. The hope of this narrative is to honor the Lord for His faithfulness and transforming grace.

John White once made a comment that I believe could also apply to this book. "Miracles are to authenticate God's messages and to awaken our awe and reverence before Him. They are not to vindicate our personal faith. It is not by miraculous deliverance that our faith grows, but by discerning His faithfulness in the midst of our pain."

Watch this hidden miracle unfold!

—Elizabeth Heinmiller

Acknowledgments

First, we would like to give thanks to the Lord for His hand upon us as we embarked upon a new adventure—writing a book! From putting the first thoughts into writing, to wisdom in editing, to finding the path in publishing, the Lord was guiding us all the way. We praise Him!

Thank you to all our family and friends, who shared their memories about the story, prayed for us, and encouraged us. Whether we directly quoted from your shared memories or not, your personal remembrances aided us in confirming the time frames and details of the story as we remembered them.

Thank you to Aunt Liz for your joy in sharing a special foreword in our book, and also to Rev. Marc Swan for reading our manuscript and sharing your reflections.

We also want to thank those who specifically helped us in our editing: Gerald and Roberta Smith, the Tom Kranz family, Krista Grose, Tina Powers, Ali Stoltman, Debbie Vanderpool, Elizabeth (Aunt Liz) Heinmiller, Mary Gene Hennessy, and Maribeth Runyan. Special thanks to Jessica Toth for your photography for our cover photo and author pictures, and to Lorè DiSalvo for the photo editing you did for a scanned family photo.

Thank you to each person at Lulu Publishing whom we worked with. We appreciate your services, which made publishing our book a reality.

May God use this book for His glory and for the edification of all who read it!

Sol dio Gloria!

Family and Friends named in this book as they related to Catherine at the time the story takes place

~Immediate Family~

Jerry and Roberta Smith (parents)

R.J. (brother) and Stacie (sister-in-law) Smith

(R.J. has since remarried)

Tom (brother-in-law) and Cindy (sister) Kranz

Terry (brother) and Tiffany (sister-in-law) Smith

Nieces & Nephews-

Zachary, Julia, William Smith

Christina, Anna, Jonathan, Teresa, Caleb, Matthias, Timothy, Andrew Kranz

Justin and Jordyn Smith

~Other relatives~

Grandpa Bob and Grandma Dolly Terwillegar: Maternal grandparents

Grandpa Jack and Grandma Rita Smith: Paternal grandparents

Edna: great-aunt (Mom's Side)

David, John, Karen, Joe, Peggy, Mary Kay: Dad's siblings

Bettye, Elaine: Mom's siblings

~Friends~

Family friends: Charles and Liz Heinmiller, Phyllis Snavely

Church friends: Mary Virginia Hill, Bjorna Rennie, Rod and Judy Graham, Jerry and Sherry Trenkler, Carolyn Tuke, Barb Kling, Barbara Ford, Gene Michael, Wayne and Sonya Shelton, Miriam Owens (priest), Murphy Family

Community Bible Study Friends: Nancy Templeman, Marilyn Pelton, Laura Osterhoff, Gerry & Linda Meadows, Debbie Vanderpool, Andrea Peterson, DeeDee Hopfinger, Pam Bassette

High School friends: Pam Fields Rossi, Lisa Driemiller, Kathy Moore

Long Lake Teacher Friends: Dean & Donna Pohl, Barbara Hollenbeck, Mary Hall, Elaine Lamporte, Monica Parent, Bernie Keller

Charlotte School Friends: Barbara Agor, Lori Anderson, Charlie Avino, Juanita Battles, Bonnie Bush, Mary Kay Dimino-Lara, Margie Hastings, Betsy Hoffer, Tricia Wenner,

~Doctors ~

Dr. Torres: Emergency Room Doctor

Dr. Bavibidila: Medical Doctor

Dr. Honch: Neurologist

Christina (Hanss) McKay: Orthotist

~Therapists~

Molly Deweese: Speech Therapist

Marlena, Amy, Keri: Hospital Therapists

Karen, Jen, Kathleen, Tricia, Nancy: Rochester Rehab Outpatient therapists

Note: The Friends box includes those directly named in the book, but is by no means an exhaustive list of Catherine's dear friends.

1

It was Thursday, April 1, 1999. I decided to take a personal sick-day from my job as a teacher at Charlotte Middle School in Rochester, New York. A trip to my doctor the day before had confirmed that the illness I had been fighting for a few days was more than an annoying virus; it was bronchitis. I had severe asthma which only complicated such illnesses for me. I spent that Thursday resting and sleeping, waiting for the medication to take effect.

In the evening I went to the tanning salon. My sister-in-law, Tiffany, was also there. She was going to the hospital for gallbladder surgery the next morning, and I told her that I would be praying for the surgery to go well. We talked and laughed together as usual before saying good-bye. I never guessed that would be our last conversation using normal communication.

When I arrived at home, I called my sister, Cindy.

"What are you doing for Easter?" I asked.

"Why don't you come here?" she said. "You could come tomorrow afternoon and spend the weekend with us, since Mom and Dad won't be back from North Carolina."

"That sounds good." We talked for a little while about a variety of subjects like sisters do. "Something funny is happening to me," I admitted. "I have been bumping into walls. Maybe it is from the medication I am taking for this bronchitis. I just feel weird."

After that conversation, I called Betsy, a friend from Charlotte Middle School. I told her that I would see her the next day at work. Our area had received so much snow that winter that the school had used too many snow days to get all of Good Friday off. There would be a half day of school, and I decided to go. I was feeling okay and thought I should make the effort.

Around ten o'clock, I went upstairs to bed. I lay down and was praying when the right side of my body felt funny to me.

What is happening to me? I wondered.

I tried to stand up, but I couldn't. I was living in my parents' home at the time, but since they were still away on vacation, I was alone. With all my strength, I dragged myself into my parents' room across the hall to get the phone so I could call for help. Looking at the phone in my hand, I was shocked to find that I couldn't read anything on it. In deep frustration I threw the phone across the room. I started to leave my parents' room, but I hadn't gotten very far before dragging myself along was more than I had strength for. All I could do was wait.

As I lay there, I began thinking and talking to God. "God, I feel Your peace in my heart right now. I know that maybe soon I will be with You in heaven, or You will send someone to help me."

My heart was totally at peace with what was happening, even though in later days I struggled to accept my condition and changed life. I truly experienced what Philippians 4:6–7 says: "Do not be anxious about anything, but in everything by prayer and supplication with thanksgiving let your requests be made known to God. And the peace of God, which surpasses all understanding, will guard your hearts and your minds in Christ Jesus."

I remember seeing a bright light shining in the distance before everything went black. I later learned that I lay there alone and unconscious for ten hours.

I don't remember anything during that time or for the next few weeks, but I have been told many things that put the pieces of the story together for me.

Betsy arrived at school on Good Friday, and knowing that I was coming in for the day, she thought it odd that I wasn't in my room yet. I was usually at work early … definitely before she was!

Catherine is always on time, she thought. *I wonder what happened. Maybe her alarm just didn't go off.*

In any case, she had to find out for sure why I wasn't where I said I'd be. She decided to come to my house, thinking again, *She'll probably just kick me out and tell me her alarm didn't go off on time.*

But I didn't answer her knock. I didn't "just kick her out." The house was locked and dark, and the newspaper was still on the front step—all signs that no one had left the house that morning. Betsy walked two doors down to our neighbors', the Lavens', so she could call the police and my younger brother, Terry, who she knew lived less than five minutes away.

Terry later recounted his experiences during that morning:

It was the morning that my wife, Tiffany, was going into the hospital for gallbladder surgery, and we were in the car ready to leave when the phone rang. Tiffany insisted that I should answer the phone. It was Catherine's friend from school. She said that the police were at Mom and Dad's house. Catherine had not shown up for work, her car was in the driveway, and the doors were locked. Tiffany went to the hospital by herself while I went to see about Catherine.

I don't remember whether I had a key or broke into my parents' house. (The police would not break in, because they could not see Catherine in trouble or hurt.) When we all went into the house, the police officers, Catherine's friend, and I found Catherine on the floor of Mom and Dad's room. She had vomited, was blue, wasn't breathing well, and wasn't coherent. The police called an ambulance immediately.

At first I assumed that Catherine had taken too much medication or was just really sick. I never imagined it was a stroke! I was really scared for Catherine. I thought about how she must have been scared being all alone, not knowing what was wrong with her and not having anyone to help her. I was later upset with myself for even thinking Catherine had taken too many pills. I knew she had been depressed, had a cold, and was out of work for a couple of days, so I didn't know what to think about all the pills and medicine I found at the house.

Mom and Dad were in North Carolina visiting the Heinmillers

(our family's longtime friends, who were like another aunt and uncle to us). I called Mom and Dad to let them know what had happened.

I followed the ambulance to Rochester General Hospital's Emergency Department, where the doctors asked me many questions about Catherine, her health, and all the meds she was taking.

The doctors started doing all their tests to find out what was wrong with her. I called Mom and Dad again after the doctors told me that Catherine was very sick and was getting worse. I called my siblings, Cindy and R.J., and our aunt Elaine. By late morning they were all at the hospital with me.

My mom, Roberta, remembers Good Friday this way:

We were visiting our friends Charles and Liz Heinmiller in Chapel Hill, North Carolina, and received the call from our son, Terry, on Good Friday morning. He said that something had happened to Catherine. He was standing in our bedroom, and Catherine was lying on the floor while he was talking with us. Catherine's friend Betsy was also there, as she was the one who had initiated the search of the house for Catherine. The ambulance was on its way.

I immediately called Nancy Templeman, who was our prayer chairman for Community Bible Study (CBS) Leaders Council, and asked her to get the prayer chain going. Shortly after that, we received another call saying Catherine was in critical condition in the hospital. Unfortunately our car was in the garage being fixed; otherwise, we would have been on our way home immediately. Our friend Liz offered us her car to use, and we left for Rochester as soon as we were packed. We expected to arrive around 11:30 p.m.

It was an extremely anxious trip. Several times we received calls saying that the doctors weren't sure if Catherine was going to make it. We prayed that God would be merciful to her and to us, and that we would make it back in time to see her.

Just that morning, I had been reading the scripture about Jesus's mother standing by the cross as her son suffered such agony. Part of being a mother is sharing in the suffering of your children. I had also been reading about Jesus healing the blind man, and Jesus's disciples wondering whether the sin of the man or his parents had caused the blindness. Jesus replied that this was for God's glory and not because of someone's sin. I received this as a word of comfort for all of us that God would use this suffering for His glory.

❖   ❖   ❖   ❖

Another excerpt from Terry:

Throughout the day, in between conferring with the doctor for Catherine, I called Strong Hospital to tell Tiffany what was going on. Later, after her surgery, I talked to her doctors. Her parents had kindly joined her at the hospital, since I couldn't be there. She was recovering well and could return home within a couple days.

❖   ❖   ❖   ❖

Catherine speaks again:

All my siblings and my aunt arrived at the hospital within an hour or so. Mom and Dad lived the longest twelve hours of their lives driving back to New York, wondering if they would make it to see me one last time. Although they had a cell phone, it was not very reliable. Nor did it have good reception. They called several times, but because of the phone issues they had limited communication with my siblings. They heard enough to know that I was still alive but in critical condition.

Dr. Torres was my emergency room doctor. He notified my primary doctor, Dr. Bavibidila, began ordering tests, and requested a consultation with the head neurologist, Dr. Honch. Upon examination, I was unresponsive, but Dr. Torres and his team determined that I had an intracerebral bleed. Dr. Honch's observations were thorough and bleak:

~I was lying on the bed mute.

~My eyes were rolled to the left and back to the midline and didn't respond to threats. However, the pupils responded to bright lights.

~I followed no commands.

~I had right-side facial weakness.

~ I vomited bilious material.

~I spontaneously would make purposeful movements with my left hand or leg. That type of movement versus sporadic nerve movement indicated severe brain injury.

The CAT scan showed a large, deep intracerebral hemorrhage—a type of stroke—with massive effects. There was a three-millimeter left-to-right midline shift and a small hemorrhage into the lateral ventricle as well. Dr. Honch's plan was to perform an angiogram of the brain, support healing as best as possible in the intensive care unit, and intubate if necessary. The doctors ruled out surgery because the bleed was so deep and the brain is so delicate. There were more tests to perform and information to glean, but no treatment could be given to correct any damage. They said the effects were clearly irreversible.

And so my family gathered together, waited—and prayed.

The exact size of the large, deep

intracerebral hemorrhage

on the left side of my brain

4 cm x 7 cm

(About the size of a business card)

2

My niece, Anna, eleven years old at the time, shares:

It was about ten o'clock Good Friday morning, and I was in the kitchen making a batch of Easter cookie dough. Suddenly my father, Tom, came to my mother, Cindy, who was near the kitchen. He had a concerned expression on his face.

He said, "I don't know when the phone rang or how we missed it, but Mom Smith left a message on the answering machine saying that Catherine was found unconscious this morning."

I stopped what I was doing. My heart must have skipped a beat. I felt horrible. *My aunt, unconscious?* I tried as hard as I could to picture her—a lovable, kind, active person—lying unconscious. I couldn't imagine her lying in a hospital bed in the emergency room.

Grandpa and Grammy Smith had been down south in North Carolina for a two-week vacation visiting very dear family friends. That two-week period was up this very day. They should have been home, but they had car trouble and were going to come home a few days later than planned once the car was fixed.

After we received the phone message, Mommy called Grammy back to get more information. There wasn't much, except that she and Grandpa were packing up and would drive back in Aunt Liz's car. Soon after that, Uncle Terry called to inform us as well.

Uncle Terry had found Aunt Catherine unconscious in Grandpa and Grammy's room. The EMTs were able to bring her to consciousness for only a short time. They took her to the emergency room at Rochester General Hospital, and the doctors were doing CAT scans and other tests.

With all of this shocking and serious information, we quickly made plans for Mommy to go to the hospital immediately. The rest of us would follow after she called us with more information. Mommy grabbed some lunch and her Bible, and she was out the door. From that point on, the phone was constantly in use. Uncle Terry couldn't reach Uncle R.J., so Daddy tried a couple times and finally got through. We also called to ask our church friends—the Durkees, Mattes, and Stellpflugs—to be praying. I was setting out an easy lunch that everyone could eat as they were able to when the phone rang again. We could tell it was Uncle Terry, and all of us stopped to listen.

When Daddy got off the phone, he turned to us and said, "Aunt Catherine had a brain hemorrhage. She isn't talking, and she's paralyzed on her right side. The doctors said the damage is irreversible." He turned his head and wept. He couldn't say anything more, and neither could we.

There was a lump in our throats and an ache in our hearts. Would the Lord save her life and restore what she had lost? We didn't know what would happen.

Since none of us felt like eating after that, we busied ourselves with packing pajamas for everyone, pillows, sleeping bags, a diaper bag, and things to do.

Christina, Anna's fourteen-year-old sister, shares her perspective:

As soon as my mom left for the hospital, my sister set a "get-it-yourself" lunch on the counter. We wanted to be ready to go to Rochester when Mommy called us. So everyone scrambled to finish what they were doing. No one was really thinking about anything except Aunt Catherine. No one felt like eating or doing anything. In fact, I am not quite sure what everyone did during that hour of silence. I only know what I did. I tackled the job of unpacking the van! Our van was packed full of bottled water, in boxes, just purchased the night before. This was not the first time I had done this particular job. I just did not feel like doing anything. My heart was somewhere else, a long way away. But the job had to be done. I grabbed a cold oat burger as I headed out to the van.

One, two, three boxes. I poked my head into the kitchen. No call yet. Those boxes seemed like they were one hundred pounds instead of fifty. They jostled against me as I walked up the hill, around the house, down the concrete basement stairs, and to the pile of other water boxes. All the while, my mind followed a turbulent stream. *Will she be okay? I hate carrying these boxes! Only three more. I wonder if Mommy is there yet. Blah! Cold oat burgers! They are usually so delicious, but today they taste like cardboard!* But I wouldn't have known what else to eat. Nothing sounded appetizing. I just did not feel like eating. *When will we know what's happening? Will Aunt Catherine be okay? Done!* I slammed the van door shut and closed the bulkhead doors of the basement. Then I headed inside, relieved—but not happy.

Daddy was on the phone when I stepped in the back door. My stomach knotted. I don't know why. I had been waiting for this call with each step of my drudgery. I held my breath.

When Daddy got off the phone, he started to say that we should get our things together. But nothing more came out. I didn't often see my father cry. It stopped me short. Then he choked, "Aunt Catherine had a brain hemorrhage, she is in serious condition, and they don't know …" I didn't need to hear more, though I waited. We were going.

Things moved quickly after that. We packed baby things for Matthias (my six-month-old brother), some food, and pajamas. Pajamas? I turned around when I heard that item mentioned. Would we spend the night? What about the animal chores? Suddenly, though, the animals weren't important. We could figure out that detail tonight. All we wanted to do was get up to the hospital.

My sister packed up bedding and other things for sleeping over. We would camp out at my grandparents' house if needed. Daddy changed Matthias's diaper. I guessed we were ready to go. Then I remembered lunch. Turning around, I surveyed the forgotten meal.

Oat burgers. Had any food ever been so unappetizing? I shoved them into the refrigerator. I was on my way to Rochester. I had to see Aunt Catherine.

Anna:

Daddy and we six children arrived at the hospital around 12:30 p.m. Uncle R.J. and Aunt Stacie were there, as were Uncle Terry, Aunt Elaine, and her friend Bruce. Many of Aunt Catherine's teacher friends from Charlotte Middle School were present too.

It wasn't a cold day, but I couldn't help shivering. Uncle R.J. and Aunt Stacie were outside the hospital when we arrived. Aunt Stacie stayed with us children while Daddy and Uncle R.J. went inside. She was very kind and engaged us in conversation.

Christina:

When we arrived at the hospital, my uncle R.J. and his wife, Stacie, greeted us in the parking lot. Their faces were somber.

"The hemorrhage is in the left side of her brain. She's unconscious, and she hasn't moved her right side," was their update.

My mind tumbled at the thought. I didn't know yet what the significance of a left-sided hemorrhage was. All I gleaned from their conversation was that she might not talk again. She might not hear well again, and she might have problems understanding us—if she pulled through. Also, the doctors were concerned about paralysis on her right side. She was still in the emergency department, awaiting admittance to the intensive care unit.

"They are letting family go in," my uncle offered to my dad. "I'll show you the way."

My dad went along with my uncle, while my aunt stayed out in the van with us.

❖   ❖   ❖   ❖

My brother-in-law, Tom, shares:

I remember going in to see Catherine in the emergency room. She was hooked up to all sorts of medical apparatus. I could tell she was unresponsive to any of my attempts to communicate with her, but I continued to talk to her. A nurse came to check something and encouraged me to keep talking. I held Catherine's hand and prayed for her aloud. I told her about all the people who were here to see her, caring for her. Then I began singing one of the songs she had written, "The Creation Song." I was unable to finish, however, as the tears flowed.

The Creation Song

{chorus}
    Oh the birds are God's orchestra.
    And they sing the creation song.
    While the Lord conducts them,
    They sing their song loud and strong.
    They sing the creation song.

{verse 1}
    There is always music to be heard
    If your heart is quiet and still.
    The trees will carry their melodies
    As the sound keeps growing full.

{verse 2}
    Listen to the birds in their beauty.
    Listen to their melodies.
    Can you hear their sweet harmony
    As they sing God's symphony?

Christina:

Out in the parking lot with my siblings and aunt, I noticed our aunt was dressed in her working "duds."

"We were going to paint the bathroom today, since we both had the day off," she explained. "When we heard about Aunt Catherine, we just dropped everything and came, not even stopping to change first!"

I smiled; everyone had dropped their plans like we did.

"Where are our cousins?" we asked.

"They were spending the day with friends since we were planning to paint, and we didn't bring them when we came here," she said.

Her kind, quiet talking distracted us and helped to calm our anxieties. She told us funny things and even got us to smile. I have always looked back on that as one of the most helpful aspects of that horrible day. Life does contain many interesting and amusing things, and it continues to go on even in the midst of a crisis.

The one thing I particularly remember is when she found out that Caleb, my twenty-month-old brother, called my sister Teresa "Te-Te."

"You stole my name!" my aunt exclaimed. "All of my nieces and nephews on my family's side can't say "Stacie." Instead, they call me "Te-Te!" In spite of our heartache and uncertainty, we found ourselves entertained and even cheerful.

Though a cloud still hung over our hearts, we were helped by the presence of my aunt Stacie's kind entertainment. I think I learned a lesson about helping people in their times of distress. Just a kind word, a listening ear, and a selfless attitude can be the greatest gifts in hard times.

By this time it was well past noon. Dr. Honch met with my family and said that I was in critical condition and might not survive. Even if I did survive, the damage would be irreversible. My right side was paralyzed completely, and the portions of my brain that controlled my speech were greatly affected. He said that they should consider what my quality of life would be.

My family's minds were whirling. *Quality of life? As in, choose either to end her life or not at this point?* There was no conclusion yet that I was considered brain-dead, although I was unconscious and recovery was not promising. Nevertheless, there was still hope in the Lord.

Lamentations 3:21–27 says, "But this I call to mind, and therefore I have hope: The steadfast love of the Lord never ceases; his mercies never come to an end; they are new every morning; great is your faithfulness. 'The Lord is my portion,' says my soul, 'therefore I will hope in him.' The Lord is good to those who wait for him, to the soul who seeks him. It is good that one should wait quietly for the salvation of the Lord. It is good for a man that he bear the yoke in his youth."

Anna:

After about twenty to twenty-five minutes, Daddy and Mommy came out and Aunt Stacie went inside the hospital.

"It is very serious," Mommy told us through tears. "It is life-threatening."

They asked if any of us wanted to go in and see Aunt Catherine. Christina and I both wanted to, so Daddy took us in while Mommy fed Matthias, who was just six months old. Juanita, from Charlotte Middle School, was leaving as we were approaching the entrance. She waved to us, and I saw the unmistakably sad look on her face. I didn't meet everyone personally, but Daddy acknowledged Aunt Catherine's colleagues sitting in the waiting room. There were several of them.

Daddy took me in to the cubicle where Aunt Catherine lay while Christina waited with the others, as there wasn't room for more than a few people to go in at a time. When I saw my aunt, she was on her back looking as though she were sleeping—except that her eyes fluttered often. Sometimes she made restless movements with her left leg, but her right side was motionless. I was glad to see her because it helped me to not imagine the situation to be worse than it was. Yet, just because it was good for me to see her, it did not mean it wasn't hard for me to see her in this condition … it was harder than words can explain. The tragedy was real. It really was happening to *my* aunt. I had not experienced anything like it before in my eleven years of life.

A medical professional came in just then.

"We are going to take Catherine for another test now," she explained. "Then she will be admitted to the intensive care unit. You will all need to leave, and any others who want to visit her will have to wait until we come to the ICU waiting room to get you after she is settled in a room."

We all found our way up to the ICU waiting room, and we sat there for an hour or two. The priest, Miriam, from Aunt Catherine's church came to the hospital, and Betsy was still with us, too. All we could do was wait and visit. Uncle Terry left to go visit Aunt Tiffany at Strong Memorial Hospital as she recovered from her surgery, and then he came back in the late afternoon. Occasionally, someone would try to call Grandpa and Grammy on their cell phone, but the connection was horrible. They were still a long way from Rochester and wondered how much time they had to make it. No one knew. We could only tell them what Aunt Catherine's current condition was.

Finally, we were told that Aunt Catherine was in her room and we could go in to see her, two or three people at a time. When I saw her again, she was lying flat in her bed and resting peacefully, but totally unresponsive. I wished she would open her eyes and see me. I wanted to see her smile or hear her voice again. But I rejoiced that she was still with us and God was in control, even in this.

Christina:

How long can a day last? It all depends upon what is contained in it. When I was waiting to see my aunt in ICU, it seemed like a day passed.

The priest, Miriam, from my aunt's church came to the hospital. She was visiting pleasantly with us all. But when someone mentioned how the stroke might affect Aunt Catherine, her face paled. "I had only heard she was in the hospital," she said. "I thought this was another asthma attack! I had no idea she was so seriously ill!"

When it was my turn to see Aunt Catherine, I went in with Miriam and my uncle. The room was dark. Monitors were beeping, and the smell of antiseptic permeated the air. As I turned the corner to face my aunt, I realized that she was still there. I had been preparing more or less to say "good-bye," but she was still alive. A flood of relief washed over me!

I touched her arm and whispered, "Hi, Aunt Catherine. It's Christina. I love you!"

To my amazement, she turned over and looked at me, though it seemed maybe she looked right through me. She reached over toward me, but she then dropped her hand, ran her fingers through her hair, and closed her eyes. Her body would not rest. Her left leg was constantly moving up and down.

Miriam leaned over her and began to pray. I joined in and felt the peace that passes understanding flood my mind.

Anna:

Around 4:00 p.m. our family decided to go to Grammy and Grandpa Smith's house to eat dinner and let the little ones play. It was hard to leave, but we needed to take care of ourselves too. It had been a long day of waiting and sitting.

It was strange to go to Grandpa and Grammy's house and not have them or Aunt Catherine there, but we made ourselves at home and were able to relax a little bit. We didn't feel hungry even though it was dinnertime, but once we thought about it long enough, we realized that we had used more energy than we imagined. Daddy called a few of our friends, as well as some of Grammy and Grandpa's, to share with them and ask for prayer. Then he called the Durkees to see if they could go to our house to feed the chickens and to put our dog, Biscuit, in the shop for the night. They were glad to help and assured us of their prayers. Mommy cleaned up Grammy and Grandpa's room where Aunt Catherine had gotten sick, while the rest of us placed sleeping bags and blankets out on the living room floor for our beds.

We all wanted to be at the hospital when Grammy and Grandpa arrived, but we also knew it would be too late for us children. It had already been a long day. Daddy and Mommy wanted to go back to the hospital for an hour or two while leaving us children at home to rest and be quiet, but we were not comfortable staying there alone, given the unfamiliar area during nighttime. After a call to Mrs. Snavely, a good family friend who lived nearby, she happily agreed to stay with us while Daddy and Mommy were gone.

It was wonderful to have Mrs. Snavely with us because she told funny stories about herself and her granddaughter. The stories made us laugh and got our minds off being anxious or thinking about what might happen to Aunt Catherine. Even so, she also kindly identified with the seriousness of the situation and had genuine concern about our aunt and us. She encouraged us to keep praying, knowing that God hears those prayers and it's one way to lift each other up to the Lord.

After a while, the phone rang. From Mrs. Snavely's side of the conversation, we knew it was Daddy checking in on us.

"Don't worry about us," she said, "You take your time. We are all resting in the living room, and if they fall asleep, I can just stretch out on the davenport."

After she got off the phone and relayed her conversation with Daddy, I asked, "Mrs. Snavely, is the davenport the couch?"

"Oh, yes," she replied, laughing. "That is an old-fashioned term for couch or sofa. What do you call this?" she asked as she held up her purse.

"We call it a purse."

"See, I call it a pocketbook. Isn't that funny?! You must think

I've been talking Greek to you! My granddaughter thinks I am quite old-fashioned, too."

A while later Daddy brought Mommy back to the house. They said that Aunt Catherine had been put on a ventilator because she was in a medically induced coma. The purpose of the induced coma was to grant the brain a rest—creating the best conditions for healing. The doctors also said that there was a 70 percent chance of survival.

Mrs. Snavely offered to do anything else for us if we needed it, and then she left. Daddy, too, left to go back to the hospital to be there when Grammy and Grandpa arrived. The hospital was giving the family special permission to come and go after visiting hours because of the critical situation.

We all settled down into the beds we had stretched out across the living room floor. Mommy settled on the couch right near us. Almost every hour, I woke up that night and immediately thought of Aunt Catherine, which caused me to pray for her again and again. That was all I could do, and I would need to leave the rest to God.

Mom and Dad finally arrived at the hospital after a long day of driving.

Mom:

R.J. was waiting for us at the emergency entrance of the hospital to take us up to ICU. It was extremely hard to see Catherine unconscious, with a respirator, IV, and other tubes connected to her. Some friends from church, along with much of our family, were still at the hospital. I remember Bjorna Rennie, Rod and Judy Graham, and Jerry and Sherry Trenkler. There may have been more, but those are all I remember. After we had been with Catherine, we gathered together with everyone in the waiting room, held hands, and prayed for Catherine.

Anna:

Around midnight, the front door opened and Daddy, Grammy, and Grandpa walked in. Mommy jumped up from her place on the couch to greet them. I could tell they were worn out. The words I heard them say were, "Thank you for being here." They made their way upstairs to go to bed, and we went back to sleep too.

3

The thirty-nine years preceding this life-changing event were rather ordinary, but they were masterfully planned by my Heavenly Father and Creator.

Gerald and Roberta Smith welcomed their first child—me—into the world on May 17, 1959, one year after their marriage. We lived in Ithaca, New York, in a second-floor apartment.

Both sets of my grandparents lived in Ithaca, as did my mother's aunt and some of my parents' siblings. I grew up with family members nearby.

I was born only a year and a half after the birth of my father's youngest sister. My earliest memories include my father walking me down to his parents' house. We would spend a couple of hours there while his sister Mary Kay and I played together. One day at Grandma's house, while Mom was working at the bank, we somehow got into the refrigerator. We pulled out leftover spaghetti noodles and threw the cold, sticky noodles all over the place —floor, cabinets, walls … everything! Grandma had been on the phone. When she came in, she sat down, surveyed the mess—and started crying. I remember telling Grandma it would be okay. Mary Kay and I had lots of fun together, even if we got into trouble sometimes!

My next two siblings, R.J. and Cindy, were born in Ithaca also. In 1964, my father got a job at Xerox as a computer operator, so we moved to Rochester, New York. My aunt and uncle had moved to Rochester, so we were still near family. I started kindergarten the first year after our move. A year later, in 1965, my younger brother, Terry, was born.

Even after we moved to Rochester, we still visited Ithaca often. My mother's parents, Bob and Dolly Terwillegar, owned a cottage on Cayuga Lake. The family gathered there on weekends all summer long. There were always plenty of options for enjoying our times together. At the top of the list were swimming and exploring the lake in rowboats, paddleboats, speedboats, and sailboats. The screened-in porch was the perfect place for card and board games, while the side yard saw its share of serious badminton matches. And the cooks always made sure we had a lot of good food. Any day of the week we could shop at a little farm stand nearby to get fresh corn, tomatoes, peaches, and squash. We also visited a farm where we could go in the farmer's basement and pick out fresh eggs from his basket of nonuniform (and thus unsalable) eggs. With the yacht club just a short distance up the lake from our cottage, we watched many boat races. Since Grandpa was a member, we enjoyed fine dinners there. Grandpa also generously took us to many family dinners at the Raskellers Restaurant on the Cornell campus, his alma mater.

I was a happy child, but throughout my growing-up years I was also known for having multiple accidents. By my sixteenth birthday, I had visited the emergency room almost every year! Some of those visits were quite memorable!

The first one I recall was when I was two years old. I was playing on a nearby neighbor's stairs with Uncle John, one of my father's brothers. I thought he would catch me as I jumped toward him from the steps, but he didn't! I fell and cut myself right along the eyebrow line. I ended up in the emergency room for stitches.

At the energetic age of three, I was at our house in Ithaca, in an upstairs bedroom jumping on the bed. I bounced off the bed, broke a glass in the process, and cut my head on it. That incident found me in the emergency room for stitches again. I remember that cut took a very long time to heal.

Then, when I was four years old, I broke my first bone—my left arm. I was playing on the slide at a school playground on Thanksgiving Day. After going down the slide once, I ran back to climb the ladder on the slide and go down again. In the process, I hit my arm on the side of the slide very hard and broke my arm. My parents took me to the emergency room, where my arm was set and a cast was put on.

Within one week of moving to Rochester, when I was five years old, I was injured again. A man was installing our telephone, and I, of course, was watching him. He was working up near the ceiling when he accidentally knocked off the plastic globe over the lightbulb—right down on me! It cut my lip below my nose. The telephone man took us to Rochester General Hospital, as we didn't have a doctor yet. The emergency room doctors were wise enough to know that we needed a plastic surgeon to sew the cut properly, and God provided an excellent one for us. My mother held my head for the doctor while he stitched my lip.

In honor of growing one year older, at age six I was riding my bike, fell, and hit my elbow. It was very bruised and bleeding, but it looked like it would heal on its own, with a little bit of cleaning up. It did end up healing, but it has always looked different from my right elbow.

In 1966, we were visiting my grandparents' cottage, and I was walking along the beach. I picked up a pole that was lying around, and continued walking with it, pretending to use it as a musical instrument or a microphone. Suddenly, I fell forward and jammed it into the roof of my mouth. Wow! Did that hurt!

At seven I was sliding on the redwood picnic table in our backyard, and I got a large splinter in my bottom. There was no way to get it out, and so I traveled to the emergency room sitting backward in the seat of the car. The doctors could not pull it out either and had to cut it out. I still tell my nieces and nephews never to slide on a wooden picnic table!

I had a couple of accidents during my thirteenth year, when we were living in Rochester. I was biking when I fell and scraped my right knee severely. My parents took me to the emergency room for a tetanus shot and to clean out the gravel. Although they cleaned the wound as best they could, I still can see tiny stones in my knee to this day.

Another day I was playing at our neighbor's home with my brother's friends. They told me that I couldn't climb trees like they could. I, for one, thought I could, and I decided to show them. As I was climbing, I fell out of the tree. My friends ran away so that they would not be blamed. Amazingly, I had no injuries whatsoever. Did the angels carry me down?

On my sixteenth birthday I added to my list of accumulated injuries. At the time, our house was being painted, and the gutters had been taken down. I was walking around the yard in my bare feet when I felt something quite hard in my foot. I couldn't get it out myself, so I called Dad to help me. When he saw what it was, he told me to look away while he pulled it out. Even though I couldn't see it, I could certainly feel it! I screamed in pain. It turned out to be a hook for the gutters that the workers had dropped. Mom and Dad and my friend Lisa and I still got to enjoy my special birthday dinner at the Spring House as planned.

I was about eleven or twelve years old when my parents both became Christians. About five months later, I went to a Billy Graham crusade with Mom. I don't really remember the sermon by Leighton Ford, Billy Graham's partner, but it stirred something in my heart. I remember the choir singing, "Just as I am without one plea, but that Thy blood was shed for me; And that Thou bidst me come to Thee, O Lamb of God, I come. I come." I went forward during the altar call to receive Christ. A lady talked to me afterward, and I began my journey of growth in Christ.

At age eighteen, after graduating from high school, I worked at a Girl Scout camp for two months in the summer. Then I enrolled in Elim Bible School for one year. Frankly, I did not care for it very much, as I thought it was too strict. The next summer I worked at the Rotary Sunshine Camp as a music teacher. Then I went to Monroe Community College for two years, where I studied human resources, but I still didn't graduate with a degree.

Around this time, I began working as a nanny for two of my friends. One friend, Mary Virginia, had a new baby, and the other friend had four children. I moved in with Mary Virginia and her husband and baby, so I watched the five children at Mary Virginia's house each day. I continued to work for both families for five years.

In 1984, at twenty-five years old, I went to the State University of New York in Geneseo and majored in history. My first choice was to study special education, but the classes were full. Instead I focused on history. I was a student teacher in Honeoye Falls for one semester and graduated in 1988 with a bachelor of arts degree.

At that point I began looking for a job in education. I found a teaching position in Long Lake, New York. For three years I taught in a small school. Because of its size, I taught history to all the eighth-, ninth-, tenth-, eleventh-, and twelfth-grade students. My first home was a little house just minutes from the school. Later I rented a house from a second-grade teacher a little farther away. I enjoyed the mountains and the wildlife. Once I even saw a bear outside my window!

After three years in Long Lake, I returned to Rochester to attend school at SUNY Brockport in order to get my master's degree in elementary education. To support myself, I delivered newspapers for the *Democrat and Chronicle.*

In 1993, I started working at Charlotte Middle School as a permanent substitute teacher for five reading classes. The following year, I was hired to teach seventh-grade social studies, science, and reading. I remained there until 1999.

My heart went out to my students. Most of them came from broken homes and very dysfunctional families. They lived on welfare in the heart of the city. The students still sought to belong somewhere, so they made "families" among themselves at the school. It was not long after I began teaching that a group of them asked me to be part of their family. I had always wanted a family of my own as well, and as a young woman I thought I'd have twelve children! However, God had other plans. Through my many nieces, nephews, former students, and friends' children, He has given me opportunities to love and pray for far more children than just twelve.

Music was always a big part of my life. During college I wrote songs, many on my own and some with my high school friend Pam. I wrote "The Creation Song" for Pam and "Behold Your God" at Elim. Around that time I also wrote "I Can Hardly Wait" —a song about Jesus's second coming. In 1982 I composed "Becky's Song" in memory of my dear cousin, who loved Jesus and who died of a brain tumor when she was eight years old. Pam and I hosted an evening at church in 1984 when we sang and I played my guitar accompanied by Pam on the piano or guitar.

Right before my stroke in 1999, I wrote two more songs, titled "Heaven's Wind" and "So Unexpectedly." The latter is a song about friendship written for my friend Barbara. In March 1999, I was invited to perform in a variety show in Long Lake. I shared my two new songs and even recorded the performance using my sister's video camera.

I loved playing my guitar, and I also played the dulcimer and tambourine. I found music soothing, and I often played my instruments and sang in my room. I sang Christian songs, oldies, or songs I'd written. I sang everywhere, anytime, with anyone.

During all my college and young adult years, I attended church and believed in Jesus Christ. Nevertheless, I lacked a close and deepening relationship with Him. I was focused on my schooling, my work, and what I thought I needed in life. I was not focused on the Lord, did not have contentment in my life, and did not have a strong prayer life. My finances were in rough shape. I just wanted everyone to "understand" and leave me alone. Little by little, I slipped into depression and tried to find help and hope in all the wrong places. I began smoking again, and I tried dating services. I just kept going on with life, trying to make it all work out somehow in my own way.

And then God graciously intervened. He got my attention and refocused my vision. But He didn't just wake me up to what life really is about and then leave me to figure out how to live His way. He was right there, guiding and helping me along the toilsome, yet worthwhile, life-changing journey.

4

Saturday morning at the hospital the list of visitors was long and changed throughout the day: Mom and Dad, R.J. and Stacie, Tom and Cindy and their children, Terry, Aunt Elaine and Bruce, Gene Michael, Marilyn Pelton, Laura Osterhoff, Gerry and Linda Meadows, and maybe others.

My condition hadn't changed through the night. I was still in critical condition, sedated, and on the respirator. If, how, or when I would wake up was unknown—as was what condition I'd be in.

Anna:

The next morning I woke up to Grammy and Grandpa moving around upstairs in their room above us. They had breakfast before we did in order to get to the hospital early and talk with the doctors. After we ate our breakfast, we headed there, too.

Uncle R.J. and Uncle Terry were already at the hospital with Grammy and Grandpa. Aunt Stacie came later, bringing lunch for everyone. Some of Grammy and Grandpa's friends came to the waiting room to visit us, even if they didn't go into Aunt Catherine's room. Betsy was also with us again. Some people were calling her the hero, but she just said, "It is Catherine who has been true to her word for us." Betsy brought Aunt Catherine a Pooh bear as a gift from another teacher, since Winnie the Pooh is one of Aunt Catherine's favorites.

Our family needed to go home at 10 a.m., although we really

didn't want to leave. However, we needed to tend to our animals and get some rest. Mommy made Easter bread while the rest of us did our chores. We all felt rather glum and sad, and of course we thought about Aunt Catherine all the time.

I was in a coma for one week. I didn't know anything that was going on at the time, but I was later told that lots of friends and family were coming in all the time to visit, to hold my hand, and to pray. My dad called my friend Donna in Long Lake to let her and other friends there know what had happened to me. She was not at home, so Dad left the message with her husband, Dean, asking him to relay it.

Easter Sunday was an emotional day for many people. My mom, Roberta, shares her feelings:

On Easter Sunday, I had been scheduled to read the epistle at church. When I arrived, the first people I saw were Carolyn Tuke and Barb Kling. I burst into tears, and they were very consoling. I didn't know if I would be able to read without breaking down. I felt that I had to read the lesson for Catherine. I was putting my trust in God for a little thing as a sign that I was trusting Him for our Catherine.

That afternoon, Miriam Owens met us in Catherine's ICU room, and we had a communion service there. It was very special. I believe Miriam put a piece of the communion wafer, soaked with wine, on Catherine's tongue. Afterward, Miriam remarked about seeing the strength of faith in the midst of Catherine's condition as I was sharing about our trust in God for Catherine's life. That, too, was all God's grace. God gave us the strength to honor Him in the midst of a very difficult time, for Catherine was not out of the woods yet.

Anna:

Easter Sunday was a hard day. We had invited Aunt Catherine to come to our home for the entire Easter weekend, since Grammy and Grandpa were still going to be away. She was going to get back to us regarding how she was feeling and if she thought she could come. Now she obviously wasn't coming at all. Would she ever be able to come again?

Mommy was especially weary. While the rest of us went to church, which was hosted at the Durkees' home that week, Mommy, Christina, and Matthias stayed home. Everyone was so understanding and comforting. Mrs. Durkee's parents were there visiting, and her mother told Daddy specifically, "We'll be praying for Catherine."

Later that afternoon Grandpa called. Aunt Catherine's condition hadn't really changed. He said that there was a board in the intensive care unit that listed each patient's last name and his or her nurse's name. Today it read, "Smith .... Rita." This touched him to the point of tears because his mother's name was Rita Smith.

All that next week, I had lots of visitors every day. Friends of mine, friends of my parents, and, of course, family visited me faithfully. My parents spent every day at the hospital with me. Dad went up very early in the morning to speak with the doctors and spend time with me, and then Mom would come up later. They spent most of each day keeping their loving presence in my room.

Anna:

We all went to the hospital on Monday. Aunt Peggy and Aunt Mary Kay, two of Grandpa's sisters, were coming up from Ithaca to visit Aunt Catherine. We packed a lunch and drove in to Rochester.

When we arrived at the waiting room, Grammy, Grandpa, Aunt

Peggy, and Aunt Mary Kay were not there yet. We took turns going in to see Aunt Catherine until they arrived.

Mommy went into Aunt Catherine's room first and said that they'd put plastic circulation pads around her legs. She had an oxygen mask on, too, to ensure that her brain was getting the oxygen it needed. Although these were necessary things to help her heal as much as possible, it was hard to see more tubes and apparatus on her. She already had the IVs, ventilator, and a large stomach/nose tube.

When I went in to see her with Daddy, she was just lying in the bed, not really responding. After spending about ten to fifteen minutes, we were going to pray with her before leaving, but I started to feel light-headed so we returned to the waiting room. I was glad I got to visit her, though.

Grammy, Grandpa, and the two aunts arrived shortly afterward. After greetings and hugs, Mommy noticed that Grandpa was wearing a blue tassel on his shirt. She asked him what it was for. He said, "In the Old Testament the Lord told the children of Israel to make blue fringes on the edges of their garments throughout the generations. They were to look upon it and remember all the commandments of the Lord, and do them so they would not seek their own heart and eyes which they used to go away from God" (Numbers 15:38–39).

"That's why I'm wearing it," he managed to say through tears.

Just then, Dr. Torres stepped into the waiting room for a short visit, bringing us one of his favorite poems, *Ballad of the Tempest*, by James T. Fields. The poem depicts the night of a raging storm upon the sea from a sailor's perspective. Just when it seemed all was lost, the captain's daughter reminded the crew that God was upon the ocean just as He is upon the land—in complete control of all things. The morning came and found the ship safely anchored in the harbor. The encouragement for our family was that God was in control of this dark night of pain and the unknown just as He was the God of the brightest day of health and joy.

"I wanted to let you know that I'll be working nights now for a while, so you won't see me," he said, "but I'll still climb the stairs to see Catherine."

Dr. Torres had been Aunt Catherine's emergency room doctor. He had shown special, understanding care for her and our family. His wife had had a brain hemorrhage, fairly recently too, but she didn't live through it. She was put on a ventilator for three days. When she was at the point where she wouldn't be able to breathe on her own again, the family decided to take her off it. Even after Aunt Catherine was moved out of the emergency department into the ICU, Dr. Torres climbed the stairs every day to check on her.

On Tuesday, my dad phoned my Long Lake friends again.

"Hi, Barbara. This is Jerry Smith, Catherine's father."

"Jerry! How are you doing? We've been thinking about you so much."

"We're doing okay. Catherine is still in the intensive care unit with a respirator and feeding tube, and she is still in the drug-induced coma. They just aren't sure how much she will improve. It is very serious still."

"I am so sorry. I can't imagine Catherine being like that."

"Well, I just wanted to let you know, so that you could decide if you wanted to come and see her. I just don't know how long we have."

My friends did want to come see me, so they began making plans to arrive on Friday.

Anna:

Wednesday was the next time we went up to see Aunt Catherine. Just Mommy, Matthias, and I went, though. Daddy is a teacher and was on Easter vacation, so he offered to stay at the house so that Mommy might go up to the hospital as many times that week as she could. We arrived in the afternoon. Grammy and Grandpa were there. Mommy and Grammy went into the room to visit Aunt Catherine while Grandpa, Matthias, and I stayed out in the waiting room. Mrs.

Reitz came to see Aunt Catherine while we were there, and Uncle R.J. came as well after he'd gotten out of work. Soon Grammy came out to ask if I wanted to go to see Aunt Catherine. When I hesitated, they all said it was okay if I didn't go in. I was trying to think fast: I didn't want to get faint again in there, but I wanted to see my aunt. Uncle R.J. said that he had had a hard time going in too, and he understood.

Finally I said, "I guess I won't go in today." The minute after I said it, I regretted it. I realized that my desire to see my aunt was stronger than any fear of fainting. Nevertheless, Grammy returned to Aunt Catherine's room and I remained in the waiting room.

In a short while, we headed home. Grammy and Grandpa went down the elevators with us, and Grammy handed us a plate of peanut butter cookies (a Smith favorite!) that a friend had given them.

We began our one-hour trip home. We were on the expressway between two exits when, all of a sudden, the van lost acceleration. Mommy had the cruise control on, but even when she took it off, the van still did not speed up. She quickly guided the van to the shoulder of the road and took the key out. She put the caution lights on and put up the hood, knowing that is the universal sign for needing help.

That began a long wait. We didn't know how long it would actually be, but we unbuckled and tried to find something to do. Mommy knitted for a while, but when she finished the washcloth she was making, she came to the bench seat to sit next to Matthias and me.

"Why don't we memorize a psalm?" she suggested. "Let's find one that would be good for someone who is stranded."

Her Bible fell open to Psalm 40. Actually, God directed her Bible to open at Psalm 40. I didn't realize then that God had appointed a scripture for us to memorize at an appointed time, a psalm that would become a testimony for Aunt Catherine's situation as well as for our problem of being stranded. We memorized verses 1–4, but I like to remember verse 5, too.

I waited patiently for the Lord; he inclined to me and heard my cry. He drew me up from the pit of destruction, out of the miry bog, and set my feet upon a rock, making my steps secure. He put a new song in my mouth, a song of praise to our God. Many will see and fear, and put their trust in the Lord. Blessed is the man who makes the Lord his trust, who does not turn to the proud, to those who go astray after a lie! You have multiplied, O Lord my God, your wondrous deeds and your thoughts toward us; none can compare with you! I will proclaim and tell of them, yet they are more than can be told.

—Psalm 40:1–5

After about forty-five minutes of waiting, we changed seats. Matthias nursed, and Mommy and I ate the cookies and drank some water. It was about 5:00 p.m. by now. Matthias was getting restless, and we also were tired of waiting. Once, a car pulled up behind us. However, they only checked their own car and then took off, ignoring us.

Mommy took out her songbook, and we sang several uplifting songs.

Finally, after two hours of waiting, a young man stopped. He asked us what was wrong, so we explained and said that we just needed to get to a phone to call Daddy to come get us. He offered us his cell phone, which Mommy used. Meanwhile, the young man opened the hood and looked around inside. After Mommy hung up with Daddy, the young man said that he thought we were just out of fuel, as everything looked okay otherwise. We were surprised, because Daddy had told us that we had enough gas to get to Rochester and back. Through this experience, we learned that the van, which we'd owned for only a few months, had to be turned on to get the proper fuel tank reading if it had less than a quarter tank of gas left. Otherwise, when turned off, it always went up to the quarter tank mark. When Daddy had checked it that morning, it appeared to have adequate fuel, when actually we didn't have enough to get to Rochester and back.

The young man said that he had extra fuel with him and would put one gallon in our tank. It would be enough to get us to the gas station. He gave Mommy his cell phone to call Daddy back and tell him that he didn't need to come get us after all.

The young man could not believe that we had been waiting for two hours with our hood up, an obvious plea for help. He said that he always stops to help when he sees it. He was on his way home from a day of school at the Rochester Institute of Technology.

When he found out we lived in Conesus, and as he lived nearby, he offered to follow us to the gas station in Livonia. We also found out that the young man, David Goldstein, knew Daddy from school. He made sure that we got sufficient fuel at the gas station and offered to follow us all the way home, but we did not feel it was necessary. Thus we made the rest of our trip home just fine. Daddy had no idea if something had happened at the hospital that made us so late, but after this incident he decided to never wait two hours to find out.

The following day, Christina took a turn going up to the hospital with Mommy and Matthias. I felt sad because I hadn't gone in to see Aunt Catherine the day before. Since Aunt Catherine's state was still critical, I felt extra-disappointed because it was possible that I wouldn't see her again. I felt like I had made such a big mistake the day before.

Grammy and Grandpa were there at the hospital, and a couple of friends stopped in. Uncle David came to see her as well.

Some of us had made Bible verse posters for Aunt Catherine, so they hung those up in her room. Aunt Catherine still has them to this day. Mommy and Christina said that Aunt Catherine was more responsive—she put out her hand to them. Maybe she could even understand what people were saying. The doctors weren't sure what she'd understand, but we felt like she could understand quite a bit. Therefore, we always talked to her as if she was listening. We prayed with her, and we sang to her. We told her we loved her.

Christina:

Over the days following my aunt's stroke, we traveled to the hospital every day to visit her. Sometimes we all went, but most of the time only some of us went. Every day was different. The nurses and doctors were different. Even the visitors were different. What really weighed heavily upon us, every day, was the fact that my aunt's condition was different.

I always held my aunt's hand when I sat next to her. Being sedated, she did not respond. Every once in a while she would squeeze my hand, but the doctors were still unsure of the extent to which she was affected by the stroke. There were still questions concerning her ability to hear and communicate in general. Until it was proved that she couldn't hear, however, I spoke to her anyway.

When I sat next to her, I would sing or read a scripture to her. She was hooked up to the respirator, the IV tubing, the catheter, and a host of monitors. But she was still Aunt Catherine. Maybe she could hear; maybe her spirit could hear. Her spirit was alive.

5

Anna:

Friday, I went to the hospital with Mommy and Matthias again. I was absolutely sure that I would see Aunt Catherine this time if I had the chance.

First Mommy went into Aunt Catherine's room with Grammy while Matthias and I stayed in the waiting room with Laura, a friend of Grammy's from Community Bible Study. She was such a sweet lady. She said that she came from a large family too, and she was also the second oldest in her family. We had a pleasant time visiting together.

A little while later, Aunt Catherine's friends from the Adirondacks arrived: Donna Pohl, Mary Hall, and Barbara Hollenbeck. After they set their luggage down in the waiting room (including Mary's guitar), they went to Aunt Catherine's room.

Mr. and Mrs. Meadows, who were also friends from Community Bible Study, came to visit that afternoon. While we were all in the waiting room together, I helped Grammy open the large *stacks* of encouragement cards that friends and family had sent. We all got a chance to read them. I can't even count how many the two of us opened that afternoon.

Grammy then watched Matthias so that Mommy and I could go to see Aunt Catherine. One thing that helped me feel less uncomfortable was to avoid looking at the other patients on our way to Aunt Catherine's room. It was odd that while I always found the hospital, the medical world, and its patients so interesting, I was still young enough that I wasn't entirely comfortable with the sights and smells—especially in the intensive care unit.

When we got to her room, Aunt Catherine held out her hand to us right away. Sometimes she would point to the posters we'd made that were on the wall. Sometimes she'd move her left leg. Though she was mostly unconscious, she was much more responsive than when I'd seen her on Monday. Her semiconscious state was partly due to medication that helped keep her calm. Otherwise she got feisty! She had already ripped out IVs and pulled out her stomach tube. The doctors were working toward slowly taking her off of the sedatives.

Whenever we were with Aunt Catherine, we sang to her and prayed. One of the songs that Mommy sang every time she went was "The Steadfast Love of the Lord":

The steadfast love of the Lord never ceases;
His mercies never come to an end.
They are new every morning, new every morning.
Great is Thy faithfulness, O Lord.
Great is Thy faithfulness.

Dr. Honch came into the room while we were there. He was the neurologist on Aunt Catherine's care team and was a very kind man. At the time, Aunt Catherine was wearing an oxygen mask because her body still wasn't giving her brain enough oxygen. The poorly designed mask kept moving up and poking the corners of her eyes. Dr. Honch observed the annoying movement of the mask and, as he corrected its placement yet again, remarked that the three of us should design a better one that was sure to be more popular. He said that then we would be so rich that we could spend all our time on the beach. I can't say that I was especially interested in the riches and the lazy days on the beach, but I did agree that the mask looked annoying and uncomfortable. I wished there were some alternative.

Then, turning to me, Dr. Honch asked, "Is it hard for you to come here and see your aunt like this?"

"Yes," I said, "it is."

He nodded and said, "When I was a boy, younger than you, my brother had polio. My parents would go visit him every day, and I had to go with them, but I didn't like going to the hospital very much either. I still don't like hospitals, but I ended up being a doctor and now come here every day."

"And we are thankful that you do," Mommy returned.

I don't remember ever feeling faint again in the hospital. The Lord used those frequent hospital visits to my aunt at my young age to prepare me to be comfortable making countless visits to other hospitals and long-term care facilities in later years to care for my own grandparents and other elderly friends.

Before long we said our good-byes and drove home without any roadside episodes!

Donna, Mary, and Barbara spent a short time with me Friday afternoon before getting together that evening with my teacher friends from Charlotte Middle School. I had always wanted my friends from both of the schools where I had taught to meet each other. I just thought that I'd be part of that first meeting.

Friday night, they all met at Betsy's house. Besides all the talking that was going on between them, they watched and cried through the video performance of me at the variety show I had done three weeks before my stroke.

On Saturday, they spent time at the hospital with me in both the morning and the afternoon. They also shared lunch with my priest, Miriam Owens. She had been out of town when they had visited me two weeks before my stroke, and they wanted to meet her.

When they came back to see me after lunch, Mary brought her guitar in to play a song for me. Then they told me good-bye and left on their long trip home.

After a week in the induced coma, I was finally fully weaned off the heavy sedation drugs. Late Saturday afternoon, I technically woke up and was considered stable. They moved me out of ICU. My new room was on the seventh floor, which was the rehabilitation floor. I still had to be on oxygen, but I could wear just the tiny oxygen tubes in my nose instead of the annoying mask.

❖   ❖   ❖   ❖

Dad:

I was at ICU with Catherine early in the morning while the medical staff were bringing her out of the drug-induced coma. It was a sight to behold: Catherine in her hospital bed, in her birthday suit, with many tubes and wires. She kept throwing her sheets and blankets onto the floor—and I was trying desperately to keep her covered. Shortly after this, she realized that she had many tubes, wires, and connections, which she began removing by herself! First, Catherine removed the respirator from her throat, then her IV with the associated PIK line, and, finally, her heart monitor! I expect that this was about the time that the doctors decided to remove her from ICU.

❖   ❖   ❖   ❖

Anna:

After church on Sunday, my whole family traveled to Rochester to visit Aunt Catherine. When we got to Grammy and Grandpa's house, Daddy, Grandpa, Uncle Terry, Christina, and I headed to the hospital. Grammy was already there, as she and Grandpa usually spent Sunday afternoons at the hospital. Aunt Elaine and her friend Bruce were there when we arrived as well.

When I saw Aunt Catherine, her eyes were open and she held out her left hand to us to give hugs. She really recognized us and looked happy to see us! I was overjoyed to see her and to feel her one arm around me in a hug!

She still had small oxygen tubes in her nose, but she was "holding her own" much more than the last time I'd been with her, just two days earlier.

But even with that improvement, I noticed the contrast with her roommate, who could talk and walk. That lady was in a much more advanced place than Aunt Catherine. Aunt Catherine could not talk or walk. You could see she was still very weak, even in her eyes. She still had oxygen, and she got tired easily from sitting in a chair. Furthermore, she was not even eating by herself, so she still had an IV.

Grammy showed us the room with the rehabilitation equipment, but it all looked too challenging for Aunt Catherine to even try. The room also had a small kitchen and a dining room area where the patients and their family or friends could share a meal together. Grammy thought that was a nice idea.

Grammy later explained to us that if, in seven days, Aunt Catherine was not able to sit in a chair for three hours straight, she would have to leave the hospital. She would need to go to St. Mary's Hospital or Monroe Community Hospital, which were both major rehabilitation centers that offered long-term care. Neither of these was located as conveniently as Rochester General Hospital for Grammy and Grandpa, who were obviously visiting Aunt Catherine every day and were acting as her main care advocates. It did not seem to me they were giving Aunt Catherine time. It sounded like at the rate they were trying to move her along, she didn't have the opportunity to work at regaining what she had lost. It didn't appear as if there was much hope for her recovery, because she wasn't doing the things they wanted her to do. *After all,* I thought, *it has only been one week since her stroke, and only one day of her being really awake. Is this really how they work with people? Isn't there any chance at all? How can they give her only one week to start doing these things?*

❖　　❖　　❖　　❖

Christina:

It was a Sunday afternoon that we, as a whole family, went to visit my aunt Catherine. She was now in a regular hospital room, and we heard that she was being initiated into an intense rehabilitation program. She was still bedridden, and she wasn't eating yet. Actually, she wasn't doing much of anything except sleeping and looking around when she was awake. How would she ever do rehabilitation if she was sleeping? All the doctors said she should be able to perform so many hours of therapy a day; if she couldn't keep up, then they wouldn't keep her. She'd have to go to a nursing home. That seemed totally unfair to me! She had had the stroke only a little over a week ago!

When we arrived at the hospital, my sister Anna and I went into her room. I thought, as before, that I would be keeping a passive auntie company. My great-aunt was in the room when we entered, and I looked over to her to say "Hello." Then I was stopped short, as out of the corner of my eye, I saw Aunt Catherine reaching toward me. She was stretching out her left arm and trying to focus her eyes on us. My heart gave a bound. Then she recognized me! Without another thought for anyone else, I fairly ran toward her bed, stooped over the bed rail, and received a big bear hug! I was so happy, I wanted to cry and laugh at the same time. I stepped back in amazement. Aunt Catherine mumbled some unintelligible jabber, but her eyes said so much more. She even tried to smile.

Anna:

We went back to Grammy and Grandpa's house for dinner. Uncle Terry and Aunt Tiffany stayed for dinner, too. Aunt Tiffany was feeling relatively well after her surgery the week before. After dinner, Uncle Terry and Aunt Tiffany went home. Grammy, Mommy, Christina, Teresa, Caleb, and I went back to the hospital. Teresa and Caleb were coming to see Aunt Catherine for the first time. It took Teresa some courage to come, but wanting to see Aunt Catherine overcame the fear. She later told us that she thought that Aunt Catherine would have a hole in her head with blood pouring out because she'd had a brain hemorrhage, and Teresa knew a hemorrhage involved bleeding. She was rather relieved to see that that wasn't the case!

After Teresa and Caleb stayed for as long as they wanted, Grammy took them out to walk the halls and to read in the waiting room.

Mommy, Christina, and I had hoped to sing Aunt Catherine the hymn "He Loves Me." Her roommate had visitors, however, so we decided against it. We talked with Aunt Catherine and offered to give her a foot rub. She *always* loved for us to give her foot rubs and back massages—with our hands chopping across her back or with us walking on her back. That was how she liked it! So we knelt at the end of her bed and rubbed her feet. She showed us her approval by squeezing our hands.

Christina:

Soon it was just my mother, my sister, and I who remained with Aunt Catherine. I could tell that Aunt Catherine could hear us and understand at least some of what we were saying. This new person before me was some of the Aunt Catherine I had known so well, and some of a new person I would have to get to know. I sat at the end of her bed and rubbed her feet. She always liked her nieces and nephews to rub her feet! I thought fondly of the times we had used lotion to see if we could get rid of the calluses from all of her barefooting. But no, it never did work! Her feet were still calloused!

After I had visited and rubbed her feet for a few minutes, she motioned to me. I asked if she had had enough. She nodded her head!

Anna:

Grammy came back in with Teresa and Caleb and said that it was time to leave. Time had passed quickly, and that meant it was time to go back to the house so our family could leave for home. Visiting hours were nearly over. Aunt Catherine rolled her eyes at us when she heard Grammy say that it was time to leave. She didn't want to see us go. Grammy turned quiet instrumental music on for Aunt

Catherine to listen to. It made me sad to leave her—emphasized by the disappointed look on her face, her not wanting us to leave, and the music playing.

We said good-bye and gave her one last kiss and squeeze of the hand. When it was Grammy's turn, she said, "The Lord bless you and keep you; the Lord make His face to shine upon you. The Lord lift up His countenance upon you and give you peace."

And with that, we all left her room.

"It's hard to leave her, isn't it?" Mommy asked Grammy.

"Yes, it is hard. All we can do is leave her in the Lord's hands," Grammy said.

We made the now familiar way down the hall, to the elevator, and out to the parking lot.

Christina:

Aunt Catherine had a long way to go, but I was happy—at least at first! How would she do with the rehabilitation? Would she ever get her speech back? Though my spirits had soared while I was with her, when it was time to leave I felt a depressing sadness. I had never left her in the hospital while she was awake. Was she lonely? We all got to go home, but she was stuck there. Would the nurses really take care of her, or would she be misunderstood and isolated? What would happen if she couldn't keep up with the rehabilitation? I dreaded the thought of a nursing home. But she wasn't even sitting up yet or using the bathroom by herself again. How would she do it? It was evident that she was paralyzed on her whole right side. The rehabilitation task seemed insurmountable.

I recall my mother asking my grandmother if leaving Aunt Catherine at night was hard. "Sometimes," said Grammy. "But I always tell her when I am going and coming back, and I think she understands. I try to be cheerful and trust that she is in a good place." I understood what she meant. It made sense. I would look forward to seeing Aunt Catherine again; but for now, my heart was at peace with where she was. I was thankful.

Anna:

When we arrived home, my brother Jonathan told us that Grandpa had gotten out the video of Aunt Catherine's performance at the variety show in Long Lake so they could watch it together. She had used our video camera (which was a gift from her) to record her playing the guitar and singing the song she had written. That show had been recorded three weeks before her stroke, so we had not seen it yet.

Grandpa rewound the tape and replayed it for the rest of us to watch. There on the screen appeared Aunt Catherine sitting in a chair holding her guitar. Then she started talking. She talked so smoothly and normally. I heard her voice again. Here was my aunt as I remembered her to be. Then she started playing her guitar using *both* hands. She sang while she played this beautiful song she had written about friendship, "So Unexpectedly." As I sat there watching her sing and play, I felt very sad, remembering our parting at the hospital. On the video, she looked so normal and energetic, but in the hospital, she was lying quietly in bed with no voice, weak arms, and a sad look on her face. The medical professionals were giving her a slim amount of time to work at regaining any part of what she had lost. How things could change in one moment! Couldn't someone see she just needed time? I knew in my heart that with God all things were possible.

All I wanted to do was bury my face in the pillows and cry. Instead, I sat and listened to Grammy explaining aphasia and apraxia, challenges that stroke patients experience with their speech. Finally, after visiting with Grammy and Grandpa some more, we rode home through the darkness in our quiet van. I made it to my bed, where, for the first time since Aunt Catherine's stroke, I cried and cried and cried. Finally, I fell asleep.

6

A couple days after I arrived on the seventh floor, the hospital staff realized that I had been moved to the wrong floor after all. This proved to be an answer to prayer and a welcome relief to my family, who were all concerned about my not advancing quickly enough for the rehabilitation floor.

Once they moved me to the fifth floor, I continued to recover my energy slowly. I have a few sketchy memories of different times in the hospital before the fifth floor, but that is where my recollections really begin. I was able to sit up more. In time, I enjoyed the sunroom just down the hall from my room.

One day I had a visit from my high school friends Lisa Driemiller and Kathy Moore. They were great company, and they did something that stood out in my memory: they rubbed my back! My friends talked constantly, carrying on a grand conversation between them. Among other subjects, they discussed my stroke. I think I knew that I couldn't talk, but at the same time, in my mind I thought I was talking! I just could not get the words from my brain to my mouth. I recall saying, "Good-bye! See you later!" but the words were never heard.

My sister, Cindy, and her son and daughter Matthias and Anna came to see me once on the fifth floor as well. I still couldn't talk, although my attempts to talk pleasantly surprised my family at times.

Anna remembers:

When Mommy, Matthias, and I went to visit Aunt Catherine again,

43

one week after our seventh-floor visit, she had been correctly placed on the fifth floor. She was sitting in her chair and wasn't using oxygen anymore. She still couldn't communicate with us, but it was easier to see that she understood what we were saying to her. I got to see the lovely sunroom on her floor, and then we sat and talked with her and Grammy. I told stories that I remembered of times she had spent with us. She looked at me and held up her finger and seemed to say, "I remember, too!" She smiled more, although only one side of her mouth could fully smile. Soon it was lunchtime and we had to head home. Her lunch tray came, and Grammy read off the list of pureed foods on the menu today. "Beets"—Aunt Catherine stuck her tongue out when she heard that one!—"macaroni and cheese ..." Normally these were some of her favorite foods, but Aunt Catherine wasn't enthusiastic about any of them! Grammy thought that she would see if she could start bringing in food for Aunt Catherine as long as it was pureed. I think Aunt Catherine liked that idea! Real food!

It was good to see her interacting as much as she could at that point. Even though she couldn't talk, she was making faces and you could tell she was listening! I'll never forget, though, one thing she did that day.

When Aunt Catherine's lunch came and Grammy asked her if she was ready to eat, she looked around at the rest of us and "spoke" a whole sentence of garbled sounds and gestured with her hand at the same time. I realized that she was asking if we had something to eat too! While she couldn't speak the words, I could understand what it was that she wanted to communicate. For the first time since her stroke, I heard her voice! Her love and care for those around her was still shining through!

On April 21 I was discharged from Rochester General Hospital's medical care and was admitted to the rehabilitation center, located on the seventh floor of the hospital building (where they had originally placed me incorrectly two weeks before). I was able to have my own room and bathroom, which I appreciated. On the fifth floor, and for the first two weeks on the seventh floor, I had to be moved from the bed to the chair or wheelchair by a Hoyer lift. I was quite heavy, and adding the "dead weight" of my paralyzed side (since I had not yet learned to move on my own), the lift was a necessity. As it was, I still needed three aides to help me out of bed.

The evaluation from my therapists upon my admission noted that I was alert and determined. I was also impulsive! The right side of my face still drooped, but I didn't gag anymore. And I could hum familiar tunes. Although I had severe deficits in areas such as balance, mobility, speech, and following commands—to name a few—their prognosis for me was "fair."

Every day, early in the morning, my occupational therapist, Keri, would come in and assist me in getting ready for the day. She let me learn how to take a shower and dress myself while giving me the help I needed in the process. It was all part of rehabilitation; I had to learn how to do everything again with my new handicap. Keri had genuine concern for me, had time for me, and made me feel like I was her only patient. She never made me feel like I was just another person on her schedule. I will always remember that.

Everyone on the seventh floor had breakfast together in the rehab room. They had a dining room table for us to wheel ourselves up to and eat. Meals were a learning time, too. I had to practice using my left hand, and I had to be aware of trying to be neat and clean. With no feeling on my right side, I often had food on my face that I didn't know I needed to wipe off with my napkin! In the beginning of my stay on the seventh floor, I still had restrictions on my diet, since I had trouble swallowing. I needed pureed foods for a while, and then I graduated to soft foods—thankfully! Pureed foods were not my cup of tea at all!

Each day in the rehab room, we could find our own schedule for the day written on a big board on the wall. My daily schedule basically followed the same pattern. In the morning I had breakfast, speech class, occupational therapy, and physical therapy. Then we took a break for lunch and had a short rest time. After that, we were back to our therapies: speech therapy, occupational therapy, and physical therapy. After this second set of therapies, we had dinner. We spent the evenings in our rooms.

Visiting was more restricted once I was a rehab patient. We obviously had to make the most of our time, spending it in therapy. At both lunch and dinner, visitors were welcome to come and share meals with us. In between, we needed to focus on our work, so visitation was not permitted.

For both breakfast and lunch, I ate with the other rehab patients in the dining room. At dinner, I ate with Mom and Dad in my room. After my diet restrictions were lifted, my parents often brought a home-cooked meal to share, especially for special occasions. Many times, though, Dad would eat the hospital food that was brought for me! I remember them bringing a variety of vegetables, potatoes, applesauce, dessert, and chicken. Sometimes they'd bring me a soda as a treat, and I couldn't stand it because of the carbonation. They always thought it was funny that I didn't like it.

My taste buds changed after my stroke. Unfortunately, it meant I no longer liked things that I had previously enjoyed. On the other hand, I liked things that I had previously not liked at all! For example, salmon now fits my taste buds, whereas that had always been something I could not stand to eat. On the other hand, fresh strawberries, oranges, and certain varieties of apples were too acidic for me to enjoy eating. How I missed being able to savor them! After several years, my taste buds changed again and I am now able to eat those fruits.

Sometimes at night after my parents left and before I had to get ready for bed, I would wheel around in my wheelchair. I helped the laundry lady put all the pajamas on the beds. I couldn't understand the television, and just listening to CDs all the time got boring. I was used to having evening work from my years of being a teacher, and it felt good to be doing something.

One night I heard a young man calling for help incessantly, with no one coming to his aid. Although I can't recall the details, I remember I wheeled down the hall, following the sound of his cry until I found his room. Then I was able to get help for him.

As I mentioned before, I thought I was talking when I was staying on the fifth floor. It was about one week after I was moved back up to the seventh floor that I realized I couldn't talk. I had thought I was talking all along, but I hadn't been. I had really arrived on the seventh floor mute except for a few words here and there. The therapists called it "limited verbal output characterized by jargon."

Speech class was with Marlena. She talked a lot since I couldn't. I had to look at pictures and tell her what they were. I recognized boy, girl, ball, mommy, and daddy correctly, but it was hard to get the right words out. Some objects, though, I actually didn't know anymore. I would take a paper with about ten pictures on it back to my room and work on it whenever I could. My friend Lisa Driemiller would help me practice them when she visited me.

For five weeks, I did rehab. I wanted to hurry up and get my speech back so that I could go back to teaching at Charlotte. However, I had oral apraxia, and my voice had limited output.

I remember all my therapists very well. There was Marlena for speech therapy, Amy for physical therapy, and Keri for occupational therapy. Like everyone else, they quickly became my friends. If it weren't for the board that listed all the patients matched to the therapists for the day, you would never know that the therapists dealt with dozens of patients at a time, year after year, because they gave such personalized care to us.

In May, Christina Hanss fitted me for my first ankle-foot orthotic (AFO). This device supported my paralyzed leg and allowed me to walk. To begin with, I had to have my leg casted and measured so they could mold it exactly to my leg. Everything went smoothly, and I ambulated very well with it on. The only change I needed to make was to wear my shoe a half size bigger on that foot.

The doctors ordered semi-regular X-rays to check my lungs throughout my stay on the seventh floor. Sometimes they found certain conditions that looked like beginnings of pneumonia or collapse of lung tissue, due to the fact that I had been a smoker. But, thankfully, I was okay and continued to make strides toward being ready to go home!

Catherine three years old   *Catherine fourth grade*

April 9, 1999
Teacher friends from Long Lake and Charlotte
Back L to R: Barbara, Margie, Lori, Bonnie, Mary
Front L to R: Tricia, Betsy, Mary Kay, Donna

Catherine and Molly, speech therapist and friend

May 15, 1999
Catherine's day visit home and birthday celebration
Back L to R: Dad, Jonathan, Cindy holding Matthias,
Christina holding Caleb
Front L to R: Catherine, Teresa (front), Anna, Mom
(Tom was taking the picture)

Catherine
Summer 2000

L to R: Dad, Mom, Catherine, R.J., Cindy, Terry

Andrea and Anika, 2014
God answers prayer!

7

Weeks passed until April turned into May, finding the sun shining warmer and the trees looking fuller and greener. Signs of springtime and new life appeared. It also found me working hard at my therapies with new zest for the life I still possessed by God's grace. On nice days, I enjoyed getting out into the fresh air, a welcome change from the stale hospital air. One day my friend Betsy, my parents, and I shared a picnic of Dad's barbeque chicken and Mom's potato salad in the courtyard area.

My parents were very involved in my rehabilitation, as Mom shares:

As Catherine progressed in her rehabilitation, Dad and I were asked to join her and learn how to help with her transfers from sitting to standing and sitting again. We also had to practice moving Catherine from a prone position to a sitting position and then to the wheelchair. We were amateurs in this regard, and it was a bit intimidating, as Catherine still did not have much mobility. As time progressed, they told us that they wanted Catherine to come home for a day visit. They continued to train us, and when the day arrived we were quite nervous. We got Catherine out of the hospital, into the car, and into the house. However, when we were trying to transfer her from the wheelchair to a living room chair, we weren't successful. We all slowly fell into a magazine basket! At first we were startled and horrified, but then we were so thankful she wasn't hurt. We were able to get Catherine up and settled in a chair for her visit. It was wonderful to have her at home, even if it was only for a day.

People continued to reach out and visit. Our friends the Murphys were very helpful. While I was still in the hospital, they came over to Mom and Dad's house and cleaned for us. From hardwood floors to carpeting, from kitchens to bathrooms, from upstairs to downstairs, they freshened our home. Spending so much time visiting me in the hospital, Mom had little time to do other things. This blessing of someone doing her cleaning chores was a great outreach to Mom.

While I was working hard at the hospital, Jerry Trenkler and Rod Graham were working diligently at my parents' house making the downstairs handicapped accessible. They made the back room into my bedroom, adding French doors on the back wall looking out into the backyard.

The biggest remodeling needed was to put in an accessible bathroom for me on the first floor. There already was a powder room by my new bedroom, and a mudroom area by the back door between the powder room and the bedroom. They used this space to widen the bathroom to accommodate my needs. The back door was taken out, and the wall was boarded up. A nice walk-in shower was installed, a raised-seat toilet was put in, and a doorway was widened enough to accommodate my wheelchair. Our friends worked diligently and lovingly on this project for us. The goal was to be ready for my return home, estimated to be at the end of the month.

Mom recalls this time:

Just prior to Catherine's stroke, my elderly aunt Edna, who had been living with us, moved to an assisted-living residence, leaving all of her furniture and books in the room Catherine would be occupying on the first floor of the house. All of that needed to be transferred to an upstairs bedroom. Catherine's dear friends the Murphys made short work of that job for us. The downstairs was ready for the remodeling to begin.

In the midst of all this work, we were at the hospital daily, and we were making many late-night decisions about tiling, flooring, colors, etc. We were so blessed by our friends Rod Graham and Jerry Trenkler, who exerted great effort to speedily renovate our home so Catherine could leave the hospital permanently. We were doubly blessed when a longtime friend gave us a generous "quiet" check to help with all of our many expenses. We were truly awed at God's provisions during this time and for the generosity of His people toward us in so many ways.

The week before my birthday, I went home for a visit along with my therapists to check out the remodeling work on the downstairs. The therapists evaluated the project to see if it complied with all their specifications and recommendations. Though not everything was completed, the shower was done, so we could "try" that out. It passed their inspection. Keri also made sure that the sink height was fine for me.

The new double bed for my room had been delivered, so we examined that too. Keri and Amy both said that the bed needed to be higher, so Dad fixed that with a homemade wooden frame. An intercom system had already been installed, which pleased them. I would be able to ring for Mom and Dad during the night if I needed them.

Wheeling me into the kitchen, they took me to the sink to practice getting up out of my wheelchair and holding myself up to use the sink for getting water or doing dishes. They had to make sure that my home was set up safely for me to carry out tasks on my own. Everything gained their approval.

The next weekend, my friends Barbara Hollenbeck and Elaine Lamporte came to visit me from Tupper Lake. They arrived in

Rochester Friday and stayed through Saturday afternoon at my parents' home. They were eager to see me again because I had done a lot of changing since they'd been here last!

In May 1999, on the Saturday before my fortieth birthday, I was allowed to have another day visit at home. My high school friend Pam Rossi came to see me with her daughter Leah.

Pam remembers that day well:

In May 1999, close to Catherine's birthday, I came to visit. I went to her home where she was living with her wonderful parents, Roberta and Jerry Smith. Several of Catherine's friends were there—some of her dear friends from Long Lake. I vividly remember sitting on the floor in her living room. I believe Catherine was sitting in a chair. This was the first time I had seen Catherine since her stroke. Her right arm was paralyzed. She could not speak words but made expressive vocal sounds. This was one of the biggest shocks to me. I could not fathom how someone who was always insightful, thoughtful, and communicative could suddenly have her speech taken from her. I wanted desperately to do something—I wanted her to be able to sing and to play the guitar, a connection that we had shared so closely. In my own ignorant way, I thought that maybe if she sang, she perhaps could use words again. It was very difficult for me. Her mom got the guitar out, and we fooled around with it awhile. But it was a hard realization—things were not the same.

As I was coming to accept the fact that Catherine had had a stroke and that her physical body was different, I began to see Catherine's personality, joy, and spirit shining through. She was smiling! She was joyful that her friends were with her! She was grateful to God that she was alive and with us! This has been one of the biggest lessons for me: to see that in the face of tragedy, God has stayed by Catherine (something that I believed He would always do). Even more, I saw that Catherine was staying by God's side.

Just as Pam and Leah were leaving, my sister, Cindy, and her family arrived. There were Tom and Cindy, Christina, Anna, Jonathan, Teresa, Caleb, and Matthias. I was so happy to see them!

Anna remembers:

We arrived at Grammy and Grandpa's home a little before lunchtime. The temporary ramp for Aunt Catherine was set up against the landing going into the house. Grandpa had to work on getting a permit to build a permanent porch and ramp.

Upon leaving the van, I could hear Aunt Catherine inside the house. Should I repeat this? I could *hear* her voice! Though she was definitely carrying on a conversation with someone, it all came out in *do's* and *da's* for the most part. Yet all the expression and emphasis were there. She sounded so joyful and energetic. I was excited and couldn't wait to get inside!

We stepped into the house, and she was right there to greet us. Oh, her hug! It was a big Aunt Catherine hug! She was so happy to see us, not to mention how happy we were to see her. She was in her own home with no tubes or oxygen, though she was still in her wheelchair. What a happy day!

She enjoyed seeing little Matthias again. Turning to her friends from Tupper Lake, she explained in her own language of *do's* and *da's* how she was at Matthias's birth in September. Knowing the story, of course, and taking cues from her inflections, we translated her words. We had a great time visiting in a most original way.

Lunchtime rolled around with luscious smells coming from Grammy's wonderful kitchen. Grammy came into the living room where we all were. She turned to Aunt Catherine and asked slowly and carefully, "What would you like to drink? Milk or water?"

"Worry," she answered.

"Water?" Grammy guessed.

"Worry!" she repeated.

Taking up the armrest from Aunt Catherine's wheelchair,

Grammy pointed to words written and taped onto it, "Yes" and "No." She tried again.

"Would you like milk? Yes or no?"

"Worry," came the answer without hesitation.

"Are you worried about something?" Grammy asked.

"No!" Aunt Catherine laughed. "Worry!" She laughed again.

Finally they decided on water for her to drink. Aunt Catherine sat back and looked at the words on her board in front of her. She pointed to them and practiced saying them. She would look at us to see if she was right. We would then pronounce the word as it really was. "Worry" came out naturally and commonly. Aphasia was still a big hurdle for Aunt Catherine. She knew the right words in her head, but she could not get them out properly.

After a delicious meal together, we took a family picture as well as a picture of Aunt Catherine with Barbara and Elaine. Aunt Catherine had a big smile, although the right side of her face drooped down a little bit due to facial weakness from the paralysis. But how could even that make it anything but a beautiful smile to see?!

Then it was time to say good-bye to Barbara and Elaine. Good-byes were hard for Aunt Catherine, and she cried hard as she hugged each of them. We waved good-bye to her friends, and then we got out our birthday cards for her. We each had made one for her like we always did. We read each one slowly and deliberately, trying to let her catch the meaning of every word:

Dear Aunt Catherine,

Happy Birthday! You are a close and special aunt to me. I am very thankful to Jesus Christ for your life.

There are *so* many special times I remember of you with us! Like … when you, Grammy, and Poppa came down to our house for baking Christmas cookies! And you helped me with my Christmas gift for Daddy—the wood plaque I wood-burned Psalm 42:1. You were such a great help, not only then, but also when Christina and I were sick with high fevers and you came down right away to help us.

Plus, you brought us popsicles and ginger ale! You came to visit us so many other times, and you always helped in any way you could!

I love you so much! You are in my thought and prayers.

Love Always,

Anna

"Love one another." John 15:17

~　　~　　~

Dear Aunt Catherine,

Happy Birthday!

Love, Teresa

xo xo xo xo xo xo xo xo xo xo xo xo xo xo xo xo xo

Dearest Catherine,

What can we wish you for your birthday? You are already so rich in all the things that really count—a loving heart, a joyous spirit, a sunny outlook, contentment, friendship, laughter, the Holy Spirit, the love of Jesus, the love of family and friends.

The only prayer we can possibly make for you today is that some small measure of the joy you've brought to us and to others will return to you now, to brighten your birthday and to warm your heart through a truly happy year.

Hope you have a wonderful birthday! We are so thankful to the Lord for your precious life, and we love you so much!

Dad and Mom

~　　~　　~

Dear Aunt Catherine,

Happy Birthday! I am so thankful to our Lord Jesus Christ for your life. He is so gracious! You are a very special person to me. You are the closest aunt I have. Recently, I've been thinking of all the things we've done together. A couple special times I especially enjoyed are these …

- canning tomatoes and salsa

- coming to help care for me when I had a high fever
- visiting us while we camped at Stony Brook
- showing us new things on our computer
- swimming in your pool

Of course, these are one-one-hundredth of the long list of special things we've done together.

I love you very much, and I am praying for God's perfect will in your life.

Your niece, Christina

~   ~   ~

Dear Catherine,

Happy Fortieth Birthday!

We give thanks for your life and your precious spirit. You are a wonderful sister, friend, and aunt! May the Lord Jesus richly bless you with all of His eternal gifts.

We love you!

Tom and Cindy and children

~   ~   ~

As the cards were read one by one, Aunt Catherine began crying. After her stroke, she became emotional more easily. It was hard to know if the memories recounted in the cards were painful for her, since now they would not be possible anymore. However, it was obvious that the words meant a lot to her and touched her heart. She brightened up and laughed when Daddy started talking about their being so old (she was turning forty on the seventeenth, and he was turning forty the day after her). She was thrilled with our gift of a fresh strawberry rhubarb pie—one of her favorites!

Before we knew it, it was time for Grammy and Grandpa to take Aunt Catherine back to the hospital. We said warm good-byes after a wonderful day together. We waved good-bye until they were out of sight.

Returning into the house, we began clearing the table and picking up the house for Grammy. Then I realized that Grammy had music playing. I listened to Aunt Catherine's voice singing her song "So Unexpectedly." This time, her strong voice and genuine words warmed my heart. Today, the sound of it didn't make me feel like crying anymore; instead, I smiled as I listened. This was my aunt. Yes, she was still the same one I'd always had and known and loved, even if the stroke had changed her abilities somewhat. I rejoiced in her life!

8

Finally! Ten days after my birthday, the day of discharge arrived on May 27[h], 1999. It had been fifty-five days since my stroke and admission to the hospital. God had wrought a wonderful miracle in my life. I was alive, breathing on my own without oxygen, eating regular food, wheeling myself around, learning to walk, and regaining my strength. Although my speech was limited, I could talk. I was standing in awe of Him through this long journey of healing, physically and emotionally.

Looking around my room when I awoke on the morning of my discharge, I noticed how bare my walls looked. We had taken down all the pictures, scriptures, and posters in preparation for my going home. They would take up new residence on my bedroom walls. No schedule hung on the door; I was embarking on a new one.

I am going home*!* was my recurring thought. *Home to stay.*

Dad and Mom arrived at the hospital early. We got all the instructions and discharge paperwork accomplished. We said good-bye to my nurses and therapists and took pictures together. At 12:30 p.m., Dad wheeled me out of the hospital to the car. I was going home! And I was ready.

Soon, I was wheeled up the makeshift ramp at our house, and then I was really home to stay. No hospital bracelet hung on my wrist reminding me I was allowed only a *visit* home!

Despite the joy of being in the comfort of my own home, the first couple of weeks were not easy. Actually, I had a hard few months. Dad and Mom had to be with me when I transferred from my wheelchair to other chairs, to the toilet, or to the bed; I was not strong enough to do it myself. Because I could not transfer myself, I could not be home alone either. Dad and Mom also got up with me in the night when I had to use the bathroom. I would call for them through the intercom system. Mom had to help me somewhat with dressing like my therapists did. She was also with me when I showered. I didn't like having them help me so much, as I wanted to go back to being independent. I didn't understand that their help was what was best for me at the time, as I thought I could do things on my own. My own viewpoint was narrow. Due to my brain injury, my understanding was also somewhat affected.

I immediately enrolled in rehabilitation with Rochester Rehab three times a week to continue therapy, beginning the day after my discharge. The goal was always to get me out of the wheelchair to walk with a cane. Once again, all my therapists were wonderful and quickly became my friends. I was determined to do my best, and I worked hard right alongside them, although it wasn't always easy.

The first visit to the rehab center, the day after I was discharged, was a thirty-minute interview. Karen Newman, a Christian, did the interview. I don't really remember what we discussed, and I couldn't give her any information with the difficulty I had speaking. Karen and I became really good friends. Even after I completed rehabilitation, she and I would go out to lunch together. I have pictures of her family with the two boys she adopted from Russia. She later moved away from Rochester, but she still e-mails often just to say hello.

Karen Newman was also my occupational therapist at Rochester Rehab. She taught me how to work in the kitchen and do things for myself there. Today I am able to do all of my own meal preparations and baking in the kitchen—all because of Karen's therapy.

Jen and her student Kathleen did physical therapy with me. They taught me how to walk anywhere. They would take me outside to practice walking on the stones. It was very difficult to walk there, but I learned how. Stairs were the same way. It took a lot of hard work to be able to walk up stairs. My therapists helped me to see that I could do anything if I worked at it with perseverance.

Tricia was my social worker. Throughout my time in rehabilitation, she had to do five sessions of evaluations. She would ask me questions to help me tell her my story, but it was very frustrating because I couldn't talk. Tricia ended up doing most of the talking, and I listened.

Nancy did music therapy. During music therapy, we sang and made hand motions while she would play the guitar. I remember singing "Amazing Grace." I liked music therapy the best because the other therapies were so hard and took a lot of work.

Molly was my speech therapist. She was very special. She became a very close friend. One of the first things she had me do was to exercise my mouth. Everything in my body was weak, including my mouth. Remember, if I wasn't talking much, I wasn't using my mouth very much. I had to practice doing overexaggerated smiles, opening and closing my jaw, and things like that. She also worked with me to practice not only speaking but also writing. Writing was even more difficult than speaking. Whenever friends were visiting me, they would review my practice sentences. Dad and Mom helped me with them as well.

I finished with physical therapy in September. Occupational therapy lasted until October. All the therapists worked diligently to help me regain what I'd lost. Progress with the right side was limited, because it was paralyzed. Nevertheless, I had fun with them all.

Molly worked hard with me in speech until March 2000. I got stuck on words very easily. Though I tried to say other things, I could still only say one word. Molly tried many strategies to break me of that. For example, I had a time that I could only say, "one day, two day." Molly would write down "one day, two day" on a whiteboard and then cross the words out to teach me not to say them. During this time, I went from trying to talk to not saying anything. I knew I wasn't supposed to say "one day, two day," but when those were the only words that would come out, I quit trying. After a long time and hard work, I overcame "one day, two day." Now I can laugh, but it was so frustrating at the time.

Soon after I came home, Dad and Mom took me to Charlotte Middle School to visit my class. I wheeled up the ramp, and Dad opened the door. There stood my class and my team teacher's class waiting for me, holding "Miss Smith" signs. With tears flowing down my cheeks, I greeted and hugged my weeping students from my wheelchair. It was an emotional meeting.

I wheeled myself to the elevator, and we went down to the library. There, all the kids sang to me the song I had written, "So Unexpectedly"—a song about friendship. Betsy, Barbara Agor, and Lori were there beside Mom, Dad, and the students. We shared cookies and drinks. I tried to talk to them, but it seemed to be all mumbling. What I so wanted them to hear was in my head but couldn't come out of my mouth in the right way.

It was a special time at school, but it also made me sad. I missed my students and my job. My days as a teacher were closed because of my severe language difficulty. I wondered what I would do instead.

When I came home, people kindly offered to stay with me so that Mom and Dad could go out. The Murphys came when Mom and Dad used a gift of tickets to the theater. But it worked the other way too. Sometimes, Mom and Dad would leave so that I could enjoy an evening with my friends. I had a pizza party dinner with my school friends on a June evening. Charlie, Betsy, Tricia, Mary Kay, and Lori came to pass the evening. It was a great time.

Although Mom and Dad generally took me to therapy, my friends took turns as well. When Barbara Hollenbeck was in town, she would accompany me. Betsy, Barbara Agor, and Tricia all drove me during the summer months.

Things seemed to go well for a while. I was improving all the time and learning so much at my therapy sessions. One evening, I had a horrible headache. It was very intense, which was one of the warning signs for strokes. My parents took the precaution of calling 9-1-1. The medics arrived in record time, took the information, and transported me to the ambulance. My parents got in their car to follow us to the hospital. Minutes ticked by, and still the ambulance did not exit the driveway. My father sat in the car, becoming more and more alarmed, since he had been told to get to the hospital as soon as possible, and this was not getting done. He concluded that we would have gotten to the emergency room faster with him taking me than with the ambulance! When what seemed to him like an hour had passed, he got out of the car and went to the ambulance saying, "You'd better get moving! She had a stroke recently, and now has a headache—and you're just sitting here!" The drivers didn't give an explanation for why they were still sitting in the driveway.

After we finally reached the hospital, they ran tests. It appeared, however, to be nothing more than a normal, horrible headache. We arrived home very late and fell into bed.

Life went on. A supposedly lovely summer was passing by, but I was not happy. In fact, I was angry. I was angry at Mom and Dad for helping me so much. I was angry at not being able to do things that I used to do and that I wanted to do. I was angry at not being able to stay at home by myself. I was angry at not being able to talk. I was angry at not being a teacher. I was angry at the whole change in my life. And I was angry at God, wondering why He'd let this happen to me. During the summer months, my mother's father became ill and Mom went to care for him and my grandma. Their home was two hours away, so Mom was gone many weekends and some weekdays. Dad made her free to go while he cared for me and took me to all my rehab and doctors' appointments. On the other hand, I also had to go everywhere that he needed to go. I found this extremely frustrating. I didn't understand my limitations or my parents' responsibility, which didn't help my anger. For two years I battled my anger. I had always been a stubborn, independent person. Now that I actually needed help, I resented it and did not know how to graciously let people help me.

After my stroke, I was very emotional. Not only did I experience a lot of anger, but also a lot of sadness. This made me reclusive in groups, and yet at every good-bye I always broke down in tears.

Christina:

It may seem that the long haul was over for my aunt when she came home from Rochester General Hospital. In reality, it was only the beginning. Leaving the hospital only meant that she no longer needed their medical expertise and that the care at home was adequate to meet her needs. My grandparents remodeled their first-floor bathroom to meet handicapped needs. They turned the downstairs family room into a bedroom. With these adjustments completed and additional training to help her maneuver, the doctors and therapists gave the okay for Aunt Catherine to come home.

But coming home was only relocation. Ahead lay a long schedule of outpatient therapy. Weekly speech, occupational, and physical therapies were the basic sessions. Aunt Catherine had a sunny, thankful disposition through it all, though she was exhausted by the day's close. She found some exercises challenging and some speech therapy a struggle, and she always felt the lack of independence frustrating. Grammy had to get up in the night to help Aunt Catherine to the bathroom. Grandpa had to help her into and out of seats and cars. She was confined to a wheelchair most of the time.

I think the hardest part of this transition time and therapy was the emotional readjustment. I can well remember the first time Aunt Catherine came to our house after her stroke. She was not herself. She was a little mopey and extra-quiet. She was struggling at the time with finding things that she could do on her own. When someone tried to help her with a few tasks, she would flare up in anger. I understand better now why these things were so hard for her. She was struggling with the changes and working to find a new identity.

Anna remembers:

After Aunt Catherine came home from the hospital, we were eager to have her come visit us again. Grammy and Grandpa promised to bring her down. After agreeing on a day, we looked forward to having them come … "like old times," we subconsciously expected.

We planned a special lunch of pasta bow salad and fruit salad, and we made arrangements for moving the dining room table so that she could get through the door from our deck in her wheelchair. We had things we wanted to show her. My sister and I were making quilts and had part of the tops done. My other siblings had things they planned to tell her and show her. It had been at least two months since she'd been to our house, and we were excited that she could actually come. There had been a time when we didn't think we would ever have that privilege again.

Finally the day arrived. Driving up the slight hill, Grandpa pulled the car up around to the back of our house so Aunt Catherine could wheel across the flat ground to the deck and in the door. She wasn't walking, much less doing stairs yet.

We went out and greeted her warmly, fully expecting to welcome our "old" aunt, who loved to visit us. We were shocked to meet our "new" aunt, someone struggling to adjust to her new life and abilities—or lack of them. She was gloomy and sad. She barely said a word the whole visit and didn't break into more than a couple smiles. We knew that she couldn't express herself the way she wanted to. We knew speech was difficult, but we hadn't expected her reclusiveness. This visit was around the time she was struggling with her speech therapist to learn to say words other than "one day, two day." During our visit, when she would start to speak, only "one day, two day" came out. She immediately stopped talking and didn't try to tell us what she meant. Since she was not supposed to say "one day, two day," she did not speak at all. Talking about her visit to school or our quilts interested her very little. We did our best to make conversation and love her, but our hearts were heavy and saddened. During her adjustment, our aunt was a quiet one with no way to tell her stories to make us laugh. We knew things were challenging, and we didn't doubt that struggle for a minute. Yet we missed her exuberance for life itself and her sunny smile.

In truth, the story of her miracle recovery is not just in the physical areas she regained that the doctors said she never would. It is also in the heart issues in which the Master Physician came to her aid and restored her life's meaning, purpose, and joy through Christ—despite her circumstances. That is the miracle we watched unfold.

9

Then the Lord answered Job out of the whirlwind and said: "Dress for action like a man; I will question you, and you make it known to me. Will you even put me in the wrong? Will you condemn me that you may be in the right? Have you an arm like God, and can you thunder with a voice like his? Adorn yourself with majesty and dignity; clothe yourself with glory and splendor. Pour out the overflowings of your anger, and look on everyone who is proud and abase him. Look on everyone who is proud and bring him low and tread down the wicked where they stand. Hide them all in the dust together; bind their faces in the world below. Then will I also acknowledge to you that your own right hand can save you."

—Job 40:6–14

Then Job answered the Lord and said: "I know that you can do all things, and that no purpose of yours can be thwarted. 'Who is this that hides counsel without knowledge?' Therefore I have uttered what I did not understand, things too wonderful for me, which I did not know. 'Hear, and I will speak; I will question you, and you make it known to me.' I had heard of you by the hearing of the ear, but now my eye sees you; therefore I despise myself, and repent in dust and ashes."

—Job 42:1–6

Little by little, year by year, I have been learning to say to the Lord, "I know that you can do all things, and that no purpose of yours can be thwarted." In my human nature, I wanted my own right hand to save me—not someone else's—but mine could not. Who was I to think that I understood my ways better than God? I was starting to realize that an abundant life comes not from the abilities I had or what I could do. An abundant life comes from knowing God and submitting to His plan for my life. The process of gaining a new perspective on life has been slow and painful. Like a butterfly struggling to come out of its chrysalis, it was through the struggle that a new creature with new beauty could emerge and take wing.

Before my stroke, teaching was my life. After my stroke, teaching was not possible, so I had to regain purpose in my life. I wanted to be a teacher again so badly that it was very hard to let go of that desire and see what else God had for me to do. I had to put my desires aside and yield to His plans. Then my joy would return.

Thinking back to the night of my stroke, I recall lying on the floor praying to God for His will to be done. If it was His will for me to live, I knew He would send someone to find me. I lay there in peace knowing that I was in God's hands whether I lived or died. As time went on after my stroke, I learned to see more and more what a gift life really is. Now every day I wake up saying, "Thank you, Lord, for my life! Thank you for another day!" Just recognizing the gift of life and thanking Him for it refreshed my joy.

As the years passed, I began to see the miracle my stroke really was. At first glance, the miracle would be that I survived. And truly that was a miracle, because I was not "supposed" to survive, much less regain many functions. But I believe deep in my heart that my stroke itself was the miracle. Yes, the miracle was that through my stroke and recovery, God renewed my heart and mind. He has helped me grow spiritually. He used it to show me my sin and transform my heart to be more like His. The road hasn't been easy, but it has been one leading to eternal treasure. It has drawn me into a closer relationship with the Lord, and that is something I would not trade for all the health and abilities in the world.

One area where I have needed to grow is in accepting help from others. I don't like to have people help me at all! I had to learn—and have to keep learning—that it is okay to accept help and even to ask for help. By not accepting others' generous and kind help, I was hurting them and being proud. God used my stroke and the obvious need for help at times to work at breaking me of this sin of pride.

By sharing the burden of a dear friend, I understood another purpose God had for my life.

In the 2002–03 Community Bible Study year I met Andrea, and we worked together teaching the five-year-olds. In January, Andrea and I were talking about her desire to have a baby. She was discouraged and crying. I prayed with her then, and when I went home I was still thinking about it.

I thought of the verse in 1 Thessalonians 5:17: "Pray without ceasing." So I began praying every day—morning, afternoon, and evening. After some time, I asked God, "Why aren't You answering me? Andrea really wants a baby."

Then God answered me with Philippians 4:6: "Do not be anxious about anything, but in everything by prayer and supplication with thanksgiving let your requests be made known to God."

So I kept praying. For two years I kept praying. Here is the story in Andrea's words:

I was serving in the Children's Program as a teacher when Catherine herself joined the group.

As we labored together, our friendship grew into breakfast dates, movie nights, and shared prayer as we set up our classroom. She showed me the room in her house where her stroke happened. I saw the clock whose numbers she could no longer read just before she lost consciousness on that fateful day. Hearing her recount the experience of her hemorrhage years before, and doing so in the place where it happened, I felt a profound sense of God's hand in her life. She had put herself fully in God's hands to live or die, and He gave her a new life. It was not the life she had planned, but it was His chosen path lined with blessings and challenges to make her strong in Him. We had that in common: my life wasn't going as planned either.

I was in a painful season of infertility. Watching my first child growing up and entering school with no siblings was truly unbearable at times. I found myself sharing my deepest hopes and hurts with Catherine as we set up our room each Tuesday. Her one good shoulder was plenty strong enough to cry on, and I often did. Catherine prayed me through a journey from pain to acceptance, one week at a time. It was just the two of us, praying in our little classroom while I cried. She loved my only daughter, Katrin, like an aunt and is still like family to her. I was quickly learning that although you can set out to help Catherine, she helps you so much more.

After I had been teaching five-year-olds with Catherine for several years, God called me to be director of the CBS Children's Program, and our teaching partnership ended. I was trained by the national organization and began preparing for the new school year. It was late August when I found out, of all things, that I was pregnant! After almost eight years of waiting and three years of no longer even asking God for it, He gave me the desire of my heart. It was so much fun to tell Catherine because I knew her giant laugh would hit the roof of heaven itself. I was not disappointed. Then, in typical Catherine fashion, she said, "Of course. *I pray!*" And I knew she had. I knew she never ever stopped, even though I did.

Catherine is so faithful—in friendship, in service, and in prayer. I really think God gave me Anika not because I deserved her, but because Catherine's faithful prayers did. I thank God for bringing Catherine into my life.

It was a wonderful day when Andrea called and shared the exciting news that she was expecting a baby! After I hung up the phone, I cried because I knew it was God answering prayer.

God has given me the work of intercessory prayer, and it is a blessing to me as I give myself to it. "Rejoice in hope, be patient in tribulation, be constant in prayer" (Romans 12:12).

As I am a Christian, prayer has always been a part of my life. It is such a wonderful gift—to talk with the Lord at any time or in any place! Through the years since my stroke, prayer has become my theme. Though words escape me most of the time, my communication with God is not hindered at all. I can still talk to Him anytime and anywhere. He hears the words I utter—and the ones on my heart that I can't utter. My language barrier with others is not a language barrier with God. It has become a vehicle of ministry to others, as I am a prayer warrior for my family and friends. It is something I can do, and I delight in this purpose God has given me.

As I have prayed for friends and family according to their requests, I have been able to stand with them and see God's answers to our prayers according to His will. Therefore, I continue in the work He has given me. I may not see the answers very quickly, but I know God is working and I have to keep praying.

Colossians 4:2 says, "Continue steadfastly in prayer, being watchful in it with thanksgiving."

10

Summer 1999 was slowly passing. For Labor Day weekend, I went to Tupper Lake. It was my first time going away after my stroke. My friend Barbara met my dad halfway to get me. One thing that Barbara and I did that weekend was to drive around the Adirondacks and enjoy that beautiful area. The next day, another former collegue from Long Lake, Monica, and her husband took Elaine, Mary, Bernie, Barbara, and me for a two-hour ride around Tupper Lake in their party boat. It was wonderful to see all my friends whom I had taught with at Long Lake and spend the weekend with them.

Meanwhile, my grandfather's health continued to decline. In August, my mother went to Ithaca once more to stay with my grandparents at their home while Grandpa was on hospice care. After six weeks, he passed away, on my grandparents' wedding anniversary.

I remember traveling to Ithaca with my father for the funeral. I hadn't seen my mom for six weeks. I was able to walk with a cane and go up steps! Everyone was so happy for me.

However, the funeral was very hard for me. After my stroke, I was very emotional and cried easily. I wept through the whole service.

After the funeral and dinner at my grandparents' home, I drove home with my brother and his wife. My father was planning to stay in Ithaca and come home with my mother after the weekend. I had progressed enough with my therapies that I could stay home independently now. Driving to therapy on Monday was the only thing I wouldn't be able to do on my own. My sister, Cindy, planned to come up and drive me to the rehab center.

In October, I went to visit Cindy and her family for a weekend. This would be only the second time I had been to their home since my stroke. My dad met Cindy and two of her children about halfway between our two houses. My speech was still limited, but we understood each other pretty well. On our drive to Cindy's house, we talked about what had happened when I had my stroke. There was so much I wanted to know about that time in my life.

I had a nice time with Cindy's family. We talked and laughed, but I tired easily. I still used my wheelchair a lot. On Saturday, we went to their neighbors' house. While they picked apples, I watched them and enjoyed being outdoors.

Later in October, I went to visit my friends in Raquette Lake for a weekend. Dad again met them halfway to get me there. Monica, Mary, Donna, Barbara, Elaine, and I rented a beautiful cabin right on the lake, and we all stayed there together. It was very hard for me to make sentences. I remember Saturday morning sitting with Monica and trying to visit. We were both frustrated that I couldn't get the words out and have a conversation. We ended up sitting quietly and "twiddling our thumbs" because I couldn't talk. Still, it was really good to be with old friends.

I remember going into the bedroom they had for me and crying. My emotions were so mixed up. I was happy to finally be able to go away and be with friends like I used to do. But I was also so sad and frustrated that I still wasn't my "old" self. I felt like a cripple.

My fall and winter were pretty uneventful—until January!

In January, I began five months of instruction at the Vocational Rehabilitation and Educational Services for the Disabled. An instructor was assigned to work with me in a type of driver's education, going over the rules of the road and making sure that I understood them and could follow them. Mom and Dad took me to classes every two weeks or once a month. After I completed the series of classes, we could set up my driver's road test.

By March 2000, I finished speech therapy with Molly. However, I had a lot of room for improvement of my speech capabilities! I continued to work at it by practicing with speech students at colleges.

Molly hooked me up with the speech students at Nazareth College. I would usually go once or twice a week, and I had practice papers to work on at home in between classes. It really helped me a lot, and it was free.

On a Friday in May 2000, I went for my road test in a specially equipped vehicle to accommodate my paralyzed side. I passed! I was so happy to get my license back. With an approved license, we could then order parts for equipping my car with the same features. I was very excited!

As soon as the work on my van was completed, Dad and Mom took me to pick it up. The man showed us everything about the new adjustments, like the left foot accelerator. I got in the driver's seat of my van for the first time in a year and said, "I will see you later!!!!" With that, I was off on my own! That was a great day! I felt free again.

The first place I went was to see Molly at her house. She was so surprised to have me drive up, and she shared in my joy!

Mom remembers:

The first morning after Catherine got her van back, she came to me in the kitchen and said, "I am going to Wegmans. Do you need anything?" It was such a joy for me to see her joy in being able to go out and do things for herself and others again.

Soon after getting my license, I drove down to see my sister and her family. We spent a wonderful afternoon together. It was so nice to see everyone. While I was there, Teresa and Caleb brought out some children's books to look at. I picked some of them up and started to try to read them. Anna was right there and helped me if I needed help. It gave me a brilliant idea! Why not go to my sister's house once a week and do "speech class" with Anna? We agreed it sounded great!

We worked at reading very simple books. Getting all the little words in sentences was the hardest part. I would often say a word for every word written, but it was not always the right word! If I got words wrong, Anna would stop me and have me try again. Sometimes I would have to look at her and watch how she formed her mouth when speaking the words and sounds. Even then, I would not be able to say what she was saying at times, though I knew what it was in my head. We laughed a lot anyway! After a few months, not only would we practice my reading, but Anna would read to me at a slightly higher reading level to practice my listening comprehension. It is still easier for me to listen to someone read or talk slowly and understand it than it is for me to read it myself and understand what it says.

The funniest reading time we had was when we were sitting on their deck on a bench reading. All of a sudden, the bench gave way! Thankfully, we didn't have far to fall and laughed over it. They hoisted me up, and we moved inside to the safe couch!

In summer of 2000, my sister, Cindy, and brother-in-law, Tom, bought a recliner to have for me in their home so that I could spend the night there more comfortably. I had discovered that it was easier to get up at night when I slept in a recliner rather than in a bed, and had recently begun using a recliner at home as well.

That fall, I had the pleasure of staying with my nieces and nephews while Tom and Cindy went to Lake George for the weekend. It was a bit like old times, and we enjoyed ourselves! Saturday afternoon, we began putting a puzzle together of a fall scene. We decided what to have for our Sunday dinner and prepared it on Saturday. We made macaroni and cheese with stewed tomatoes. We also cooked up fresh beets from the garden, one of my favorites! After church on Sunday, we enjoyed our delicious dinner. Following dinner, I was tired and took a nap while the children worked more on the puzzle and finished it—except for one piece that was missing!

That fall, I joined Community Bible Study. I worked with Debbie teaching the five-year-olds. I really enjoyed teaching again, and the little children were such fun to work with. I also enjoyed making friends with everyone at CBS.

Fall turned to winter, and winter gave way to spring. With the start of spring 2001, I started walking to lose weight. I also followed a diet plan. I walked everywhere—along the Erie Canal, at the Seneca Park Zoo, around the block, or inside the mall before store hours. Sometimes I would have breakfast at a local restaurant with Sheri and Jim, friends from speech class, before going to walk along the canal.

One day as I was walking along the canal, I passed a woman pushing her baby in a stroller. Her baby dropped her doll, which I promptly bent over to pick up. As I gave it back with a smile, the woman said, "What happened to you? Why are you the way you are?"

The best I could with my limited speech, I told my story. I told her about lying on the floor for hours waiting in peace for God to bring me help or to take me home to heaven. By the time I got to the end of my story, she was crying and gave me a big hug before saying good-bye. As I continued on my way, I realized that I did have a story to tell. It was a story of God's providence in my life. He had allowed me to live, and I wanted to use my life and breath to tell of His wonderful works toward me and to give Him the praise.

11

One of the biggest challenges with my paralyzed right side is my floppy leg and carrying around the dead weight. When I was still at Rochester General Hospital, I had to get a leg brace for my right leg so that I could relearn how to walk. Christina (Hanss) McKay, a certified prosthetist and orthotist, came to my room to take measurements and make the casting for my leg brace on May 10, 1999. They made it as tall as my knee with solid ankle joints for optimum support. Then I could learn to walk!

It might sound odd to some people, but I always say I'm all right—except for my leg. I need my leg to get around. I am so thankful that the brace allows me to be mobile. However, the brace also causes rubbing and irritation from time to time and often requires adjusting. I am grateful to have had a wonderful orthotist to oversee that need.

By August 2007, I had the brace shortened to midcalf length. I should have realized that I would need a longer brace, like Christina always said I would need, but I didn't want to think about that.

Two months later, in October, Christina was concerned about my knee being hyperextended because of the way it bends when I walk and stand. I told her that it was no problem, and I said that I could handle it.

Yeah, right! I should have realized that Christina was correct. I needed a longer brace, but it scared me to think about it. The shorter brace felt better for three months, but then it started hurting all the time. It actually did more damage to my knee because of lack of support.

After trying the shorter length, I went back to the knee-length brace in June 2008.

Finally in the fall of 2008, I realized again that Christina was right. Even the knee-length brace was not giving my knee the proper support. It needed a full leg brace, and, in fact, I was hurting my knee more without it.

When I was told that I needed to get a full leg brace at the end of 2008, I was not happy—and I was scared. It seemed like it would prevent me from doing what I was used to doing. It would cause changes in how I did things. It also meant that my clothing wouldn't fit, because of the large hinges at the knees. I either had to diet, which was hard because my pain medication made me want to eat, or I needed to buy new pants, which was also hard because of the expense. These may seem like little concerns, but to me they were altogether overwhelming.

Friends at the CBS Leaders' Council prayed for me and reached out to me. Some gave money toward my new brace. My group of friends that regularly met for breakfast at a local restaurant surprised me with money for me to buy new pants. They all are so loving and supportive.

It is a long process to get a new brace. When I went to the appointment to make the new mold, I was standing in front of the mirror and had a few tears in my eyes. Christina said, "Catherine, what is wrong?" I told her that I was scared. She comforted me saying, "Catherine, it is going to take a little time. Don't think that the mold gives a good picture of what the brace will actually be like. We're just in the beginning stages. Don't worry about the process or how we'll work it out. I will be right here with you along the way." She has been more than a doctor to me; she's a friend.

On January 8, 2009, my sister, Cindy, went with me to get my full leg brace fitted. I put it on, stood up in it, and walked in it. It felt wonderful! I was so happy and so thankful to God, yet I was so humbled that I broke down crying. God was faithful once again in my life. My worry and fear were for naught, and He knew what was best for me. After feeling the tremendous difference in the support the full brace gave me and the relief from pain it provided, I couldn't wait for the day to go pick it up and take it home.

During this time I was having pain in my left leg. Part of it was because I needed a new brace that would better support my paralyzed leg and relieve my left leg, but part of it was unexplained. It seemed that some of the pain might be due to a pinched sciatic nerve. However, three doctors suggested I go to my neurologist and get an MRI to diagnose the problem properly. It was too hard to determine definitively what it was.

A million thoughts crept into my mind. Would I need surgery? Would it need drastic treatment? Just thinking of it scared me. The unknown always makes me feel my handicap more keenly, leaving me feeling vulnerable. Surgery frightened me because it would be on my left knee. That was my strong knee. It was the knee that allowed me to walk with one paralyzed leg. How could I do it?

I immediately sent out a request to several friends asking for prayer for God's strength and peace. The next day was when my group of friends and I met at a restaurant for breakfast where they gave me the money for purchasing new clothing. It showed me again that I was not in any of this alone even if it meant facing surgery on my left knee. First, I had God, who is always there for me and is always faithful to me. Then I have my family and friends, who pray for me, encourage me, and reach out to me. I am so blessed!

12

A very special part of my life after my stroke has been participating in Community Bible Study. I began helping at CBS in September 2000. My mother had asked the Servant's Team if there was a place for me to help. They prayed together about it and then said that yes, they would welcome me to the team! They asked me if I would like to work with the children. I hadn't been a part of CBS before, though my parents had been, but I was interested in the opportunity because I loved working with children. I am so glad that I became a part of the CBS family here in Rochester!

For the first year with CBS, I worked with my friend Debbie teaching the five-year-old class. It was a wonderful year of making friends and spending time with the children. I love greeting them in the morning with a big hug and hello, and then helping them take their coats off and get settled.

CBS finished for the 2000–01 school year at the end of May. The following year, in the fall of 2001, I did not go back to helping at CBS. I decided to take one year off and focus on losing weight and getting healthier. I also tried to find a place once again working in some way with the Rochester City School District.

Starting in April 2001, I began searching diligently to find any opportunity to work at Charlotte Middle School. My friend Barbara did a lot to help me by filling out paperwork, going to meetings, and just being my advocate. She was helpful because I could not communicate well, either speaking or understanding. There seemed to be hope that even though I couldn't teach seventh- and eighth-graders science and social studies as I had before, I could be a teacher's aide.

I wanted very much to go back because I loved teaching and I loved the students. Also, I needed only two years to complete my ten years in the system, which would allow me to qualify for my retirement pension.

I spent many days working in classrooms with different teachers throughout the fall. It exhausted me, but I enjoyed it and wanted to work hard toward the goal of getting back there to work.

Eventually, I realized that I was not physically able to go back to teaching. Nor was there any other job for me to fill in the school district. I felt very sad, but the Lord helped me through that time of keen disappointment. I am thankful for the years I had there to minister to the students and be a light in one of the darkest and most needy schools in Rochester.

Once I realized that I would not be returning to Charlotte to teach, I decided to find a different job. Being part of CBS was important to me, and I wanted to be involved with the children's program that next fall. I began praying for a business that would hire me part-time to accommodate my physical stamina needs and to allow me to be available for CBS. In May 2002 I began working with a job matching service agent, Janet Nordman. She was dedicated to her clients, and she took personal interest in helping me. We began a quickly growing friendship that continues even now.

After two weeks of looking for a job and with no sign of an opening, I decided there was no use seeking anymore. I figured there just wasn't anything out there that would suit my needs and criteria. Janet phoned and said, "Where have you been?"

"There isn't a job for me. It has been two weeks," I said.

"You can't give up," Janet said to encourage me. "Come back, and we'll keep looking." After four months of persevering and having the help of my job-hunting team, they matched me with Syms Department Store in Henrietta. I decided to pursue it.

I walked into Syms and found it bustling with many customers. I went to the desk and asked if I could see the manager. The manager, Loren Romagnola, came out. He shook my hand, took my resume, and talked with me right there in the store. He didn't even take me in the back for an interview. Yet within two weeks, I got the job! My manager was great, and it was a wonderful place to work. I started working there on September 11, 2002, four hours a day, three days a week. I mixed my sitting and standing time so that I could physically handle the work. I unpacked boxes after getting shipments, cleaned up packaging, organized signs on items for markdowns, and helped another coworker with janitorial work. I loved working at Syms. I made great friends with all my colleagues. After I had worked there for four years, Walgreens bought our store and lot, and the store was closed. It was very sad for all of us to have to leave those jobs. Syms was a great employer.

Going back to CBS in the fall of 2002 was wonderful. Linda Meadows was the children's director at that time, and she was a joy to work with. I spent the next three years at CBS working with Andrea teaching the five-year-old class, as is mentioned in chapter nine. While Andrea was out of CBS in 2005 with her baby, I taught the little children with DeeDee.

In December of that year, the Lord provided a first-floor, handicapped-accessible apartment of my very own in Henrietta. My family helped me move from my parents' home. Pretty soon, I had a cozy home to enjoy and share with others.

The following year, 2006, I became a member of a core group at CBS.

I took the next year off from CBS altogether. During that year off, I was looking for another job. I found a janitor position, but it was too taxing on my body. I had to stop working in that capacity, and I haven't gotten another job since then.

The fall of 2008, I went back to CBS and worked again as a children's teacher. This time, however, I taught with Pam for two years.

I became good friends with each person I worked with throughout these years at CBS. We share so much about our lives together and learn more about the Lord from each other. In the 2010–11 CBS year, Pam moved to another class and I worked with Andrea again! I was happy that we got to team together once more. Since then, I have worked with many other wonderful teachers each year.

I am so blessed to have special friends—sisters in the Lord—at CBS. Each Tuesday the CBS staff meets for devotions and prayer. Then we also gather for prayer each Wednesday morning before Bible study commences. I am blessed by our spending so much time before our Father's throne together.

I often get together with these dear friends for lunches. I send e-mails on "their prayer day" in our Leader's Council prayer journals, or for their birthdays. They have all touched and changed my life. For several years Debbie and I met each Monday morning for breakfast to do that week's Bible study together. We both miss those times together.

I have been blessed with two opportunities to share the story of my stroke and God's work in my life. The first was at the Leader's Council for the devotional, and the other was at the opening of Wednesday CBS. On that day, January 6, 2010, Anna came to CBS, and she was my voice sharing my testimony. It has been a rich blessing to share God's work in my life with those at CBS—and to see how God can use it to touch others.

13

As I reflect on the years since my stroke, I see God's hand upon me. I am filled with praise and thanksgiving for our great God and our Savior, Jesus Christ. Every day I wake up and thank the Lord for my life and for allowing me to take this journey of spiritual growth. While it hasn't been easy, it has been worth it, as I've grown closer to the Lord. He is so faithful and worthy of my praise. He has provided all that I need and has blessed me in many ways.

One of those many blessings has been Joni Ereckson Tada's daily web-devotionals. Seeing how she lives with a disability that is even greater than mine, and yet fixes her eyes on Jesus, has encouraged me tremendously. She knows what it feels like to be in pain, to not be able to do normal things, and to go through frustration and discouragement. She shares so honestly about her struggles, but also, and most importantly, she shares about her relationship with Jesus, the rock on which she has built her life. He is the One who makes it possible to withstand the storms.

Another blessing is the love and support of my parents, siblings, and their families. I appreciate all the time they spend with me talking, listening, cleaning my apartment, going to appointments with me, doing paperwork, and being together. There have been times in my life that I have cut off relationships because of my frustrations, anger, and bitterness. Nevertheless, the Lord has mercifully brought me out of that darkness and into His light to see that relationships matter and are eternal. I understand now more than ever before that my family members are the most important people in my life. I am forever grateful for each of them.

A third blessing is all the wonderful friends the Lord has given me throughout my life. I am blessed by the sweet fellowship we share together. They are such an encouragement and support.

As I anticipate celebrating the fifteenth anniversary of my stroke in 2014, the challenges are increasing. Many things are getting harder for me to do by myself, including daily tasks such as showering, changing sheets on my bed, and bicycling at the health center, to name a few. I am falling more often, and I need more assistance. I used to bicycle, lift weights, and follow a pretty rigorous schedule, but I'm finding that I don't have the stamina I once had and I tire more easily. I have a lot of pain from the compensation I make for my right side. I needed arthroscopic surgery on my left knee in December 2010 because of the extra wear it takes compensating for my paralyzed right knee. It was a long, painful recovery, but I came through it with a lot of help from my family.

Sleeping at night is difficult because of the pain from arthritis, bursitis, sciatica, and muscular compensation. Yet the Lord uses it for His glory and purposes through the ministry of prayer. Many nights I spend hours praying for whomever He lays on my heart.

In the summer of 2011, the Lord spoke to me about another ministry He wanted me to do. Even though I have only one hand to work with, I began baking muffins for friends in my apartment complex each weekend. I pray for them while I bake the muffins, and then I wrap them up with a label that has the name of the muffin and a scripture verse. That fall, I was thinking about how I can't be as involved in the reading and sharing at Leader's Council with the Servant's Team, since communicating is difficult for me. The Lord prompted me to bake muffins for everyone and pray for them all while I bake.

Besides praying for my family and friends, I e-mail scriptures and devotionals to them once a week. I want to share the Lord with them and to let them know that I love them and I am praying for them.

Above all, as I consider my life, I am thankful for Jesus. I desire to fear God and to put my hope in Him at all times. He delights in those who depend on His power, and He loves to be the God of the poor and needy. In 2 Chronicles 16:9 we read, "For the eyes of the Lord run to and fro throughout the whole earth, to give strong support to those whose heart is blameless toward him."

My prayer is that this book—this testimony—may point to the Lord God Almighty. He is good because that is His nature, no matter what the circumstances are, and He has shown Himself strong on my behalf over and over. I pray for you, dear readers, to know Jesus Christ as your Savior and to see Him at work in your own hearts and lives.

The greatest miracle God did for me after my stroke was not that I could eventually talk, or walk, or drive, or live on my own again. The greatest, but the sometimes hidden, miracle was that Jesus Christ transformed me. He renewed my mind, He put a new song in my heart, and He gave me a clearer view of who He is and who He wants me to be. I praise Him for His salvation, for bringing me to Himself when I was thirteen years old, and for bringing me back to a closer relationship with Himself when I was thirty-nine years old through a stroke that changed my life.

~ ~ ~ ~ ~ ~ ~ ~ ~ ~ ~ ~

I waited patiently for the Lord; he inclined to me and heard my cry. He drew me up from the pit of destruction, out of the miry bog, and set my feet upon a rock, making my steps secure. He put a new song in my mouth, a song of praise to our God. Many will see and fear, and put their trust in the Lord. Blessed is the man who makes the Lord his trust, who does not turn to the proud, to those who go astray after a lie! You have multiplied, O Lord my God, your wondrous deeds and your thoughts toward us; none can compare with you! I will proclaim and tell of them, yet they are more than can be told.

—Psalm 40:1–5

Epilogue

April 2, 2014

Today is the fifteenth anniversary of my stroke. The words on my heart are "God is good." I am so thankful for Jesus Christ! I am taking one day at a time, and Jesus is with me through each one.

I had arthroscopic surgery on my left knee again this past February to repair the meniscus. My knee continues to heal … slowly, but it is coming along! It takes time, and as I keep giving it to God, He helps me to be patient.

This week my new bed was delivered. It is a mechanical bed that raises and lowers horizontally and vertically. It is so wonderful! It is such a blessing to me to have this bed and my lift recliner, which enable me to lie down or sit down without the extra pain and physical strain to get up again. I am very grateful!

I am feeling weaker and have more struggles as the years come and go since my stroke, but I am finding my strength in the Lord. When I am weak, He is strong! I am so happy in God, and I am so thankful that He walks with me!

Glossary of Medical Terms

All definitions are taken from the following sources: *Merriam-Webster's Collegiate Dictionary*, Tenth Edition; *Mosby's Medical, Nursing, and Allied Health Dictionary*, Sixth Edition; The Free Dictionary website; and The Riverside Online Health Reference.

Angiogram of the brain (cerebral angiography)—A one- to three-hour-long medical procedure used to noninvasively look at the internal blood flow and performance of vessels and arteries in the head and neck region. This procedure also helps with the detection of blockages and narrowing of the arteries in the neck that serve to carry the blood to the brain. In the event that the blood flow to the brain is either slowed down or stopped, the consequences include strokes. This procedure was used on Catherine to see if there were warnings of potential subsequent strokes for her.

Aphasia—Loss or impairment of the power to use or comprehend words, usually resulting from brain damage.

Apraxia—Loss or impairment of the ability to execute complex coordinated movements without impairment of the muscles or senses.

Arthroscopic surgery—Joint surgery using an arthroscope (a specially designed endoscope) in a small incision. This is the type of surgery Catherine had done on her left knee in 2010 and again in 2014.

Computed tomography scan (CT scan) (formerly called a computerized axial tomography, or CAT scan)—A radiographic technique that produces an image of a detailed cross section of tissue.

This scan allowed the doctors to see the size and location of the hemorrhage in Catherine's brain.

Intracerebral hemorrhage (ICH)—A type of hemorrhagic stroke in which bleeding occurs directly into the brain. The bleeding causes decreased oxygen to the brain, causing hypoxic damage as well as intracranial pressure damage.

Intravenous access (IV)—Insertion of a needle (catheter) into a peripheral vein for the purpose of administering fluids, blood, or medications.

Endotracheal intubation—The insertion of a tube into the trachea for purposes of anesthesia, airway maintenance, aspiration of secretions, lung ventilation, or prevention of entrance of foreign material into the airway; the tube goes through the nose or mouth. It is frequently performed in critically injured, ill, or anesthetized patients to facilitate ventilation of the lungs, including mechanical ventilation, and to prevent the possibility of asphyxiation or airway obstruction.

Medically induced coma—A temporary state of unconsciousness induced by a doctor using a controlled dose of a barbiturate drug. Barbiturates are central nervous system depressants that reduce brain activity, allowing the brain time to heal. Medically induced comas may be used to control brain swelling caused by a brain injury such as due to head trauma, stroke, or infection.

Magnetic resonance imaging (MRI)—Medical imaging based on the resonance of atomic nuclei in a strong magnetic field. It has superior soft-tissue contrast resolution, ability to image in multiple planes, and lack of ionizing radiation hazards. Regarded as superior to tomography imaging for central nervous system abnormalities, including those in the brain stem and spinal cord.

Neurologist—A physician skilled in the diagnosis and treatment of disease of the nervous system.

Occupational therapy—A health rehabilitation designed to help patients with physical deficits (i.e., cognitive impairments, injuries, etc.) to develop daily living skills that are important for functional independence and well-being.

Orthotist—A person who designs, fabricates, and fits braces or other orthopedic appliances prescribed by physicians.

Orthotic—The design and use of external appliances, such as a leg brace, to support a paralyzed muscle, promote a specific motion, or correct a musculoskeletal deformity.

Physical therapy—The treatment of disease, injury, etc., by physical means, as by exercise, massage, etc.

Respirator—An apparatus to maintain breathing by artificial means.

Sciatic—Of or in the hip or its nerves.

Sciatica—Any painful condition in the hip or thigh, especially neuritis of the long nerve (sciatic nerve) passing down the back of the thigh.

Speech therapy—The application of treatments and counseling in the prevention or correction of speech and language disorders.

Ventilator—A device for giving artificial respiration or aiding in pulmonary ventilation.

About the Authors

Catherine M. Smith resides in Henrietta, New York, in her homey apartment. You may find her there baking a new muffin recipe, sending out devotionals of encouragement to friends and family by e-mail, or sitting and looking at her walls of photographs—praying for the people in them. But you're just as likely to find her out and about visiting or helping someone. For when you meet Catherine, the main thing you notice and remember about her is not necessarily the brace on her leg or her paralyzed right side. It would be her smile, her laughter, her friendliness, and her love for Jesus. The light of Christ shines through her.

Anna E. Kranz is privileged to be the niece of Catherine Smith. As the second oldest of eight children, she lives with her family on their small farm in Conesus, New York. She loves the Lord and has a heart to serve Him wherever He wills. That place of service has been living with and caring for her grandparents for two and a half years; at home farming, gardening, cooking, and sewing; at her desk writing stories, poems, and letters of encouragement; and in the church and community serving young families and the elderly. She also enjoys playing the piano and serving in mission work at home and abroad.